HANDCARVED
CHRISTMAS

D1261785

HANDCARVED
CHRISTMAS

36 Beloved Ornaments, Decorations, and Gifts
The Best of *Woodcarving Illustrated* Magazine

From the Editors of
Woodcarving Illustrated

Noah's Ark Santa,
by Steve Brown, page 90.

FOX CHAPEL
PUBLISHING

© 2011 by Fox Chapel Publishing Company, Inc., East Petersburg, PA.

Handcarved Christmas is an original work, first published in 2011 by Fox Chapel Publishing Company, Inc. The patterns contained herein are copyrighted by the authors. Readers may make copies of these patterns for personal use. The patterns themselves, however, are not to be duplicated for resale or distribution under any circumstances. Any such copying is a violation of copyright law.

ISBN: 978-1-56523-605-9

Library of Congress Cataloging-in-Publication Data

Handcarved Christmas / from the editors of Woodcarving illustrated. -- 1st.

    p. cm. -- (The best of Woodcarving illustrated)

Includes index.

ISBN 978-1-56523-605-9 (alk. paper)

1. Wood-carving--Patterns. 2. Christmas decorations--Patterns. I. Woodcarving illustrated.

TT199.7.H36 2011

731.4'62--dc23

                    2011012268

To learn more about the other great books from Fox Chapel Publishing, or to find a retailer near you,
call toll-free 800-457-9112 or visit us at *www.FoxChapelPublishing.com*.

Note to Authors: We are always looking for talented authors to write new books
in our area of woodworking, design, and related crafts. Please send a brief letter
describing your idea to Acquisition Editor, 1970 Broad Street, East Petersburg, PA 17520.

Printed in China
First printing: November 2011

Because working with wood and other materials inherently includes the risk of injury and damage, this book cannot guarantee that creating the projects in this book is safe for everyone. For this reason, this book is sold without warranties or guarantees of any kind, expressed or implied, and the publisher and the author disclaim any liability for any injuries, losses, or damages caused in any way by the content of this book or the reader's use of the tools needed to complete the projects presented here. The publisher and the author urge all carvers to thoroughly review each project and to understand the use of all tools before beginning any project.

Contents

What You Can Learn

How to Use Wood Bleach
Santa with Cardinal, 69

How to Carve Intaglio Style
Santa Collector's Plate, 80

How to Create Pierced Relief
Olde World Santa Ornament, 42

How to Make an Adjustable Carving
Create a Playful Chris-Moose Ornament, 15

How to Use Mass-Production Techniques
Carving a Star Ornament, 22

Relief Carve Santa
Ornaments, 28

How to Add Texture with a Woodburner

Power Carving a Dove Ornament, 30

Passing Preflight Inspection, 96

How to Weight a Carving

Whimsical Santa Holds Your Christmas Stocking, 128

Ornaments

Ornaments have a special place in many Christmas traditions. It's more than just the colors and themes—ornaments are about memories, about people, about love. That's why carving ornaments for the special people in your life is a great way to remind them that you care. This chapter offers choices ranging from whimsical to sentimental to beautiful, for beginners to more experienced carvers, so you can make treasures for your own tree or gifts that will be cherished for years.

Dove Ornament,
by Hugh Parks, page 30.

Carving Ornaments from Scrap Wood

By Jim Feather

Tiny ornaments like this Santa challenge your imagination, require little roughing out, and take on the shape of the wood scrap.

I carry small scraps of wood and a folding carving knife in my pocket so I can carve anytime I have a few spare minutes. These miniature carvings can be completed quickly and make wonderful gifts.

Carving the Ornament

I use three tools for this Santa: a small detail knife, a small V-tool, and a pounce wheel. Carve off the sharp corners to round the blank. Mark the bottom of the nose, the center of the eyes, and the edges of the beard with a pencil. Using a detail knife, cut in the facial features and shape the beard and hat. Add texture to the beard, hat trim, and ball with a small V-tool. Roll a small metal pounce wheel around the red portion of the hat to add texture.

Finishing the Ornament

Thin acrylic paint with water to the consistency of a stain. Apply the colors from light to dark. Use white for the beard and fur trim and dark flesh for the face.

Apply a coat of black, thinned extensively with water, to the textured hat. Dry the black with a hair dryer. Pick up undiluted tompte red with a stiff-bristle brush and work the brush back and forth across a paper towel. Apply a light coat of tompte red over the black base coat. The black will highlight the texture.

I use undiluted white, denim blue, and black for the eyes. After the paint dries, seal the carving with satin acrylic sealer. Allow the sealer to dry, then apply a thin wash of burnt umber acrylic paint to the entire carving. Immediately wipe off as much of the wash as possible with a paper towel.

materials & tools

MATERIALS:
- 1" x 1" x 4" basswood
- Acrylic satin finish
- Acrylic paints:
  dark flesh
  white
  black
  tompte red
  denim blue
  burnt umber
- Paper towels

TOOLS:
- Small detail knife
- 2mm 60° V-tool
- Small metal pounce wheel
- Assorted paintbrushes of choice
- Stiff-bristle paintbrush

Creating
Clothespin
Carvings

By Forrest Holder

These quick and easy carvings can be completed in a single afternoon. Folks love receiving a handcarved gift, and the novel use of ordinary clothespins doubles the fun!

The completed clothespin carvings can be clipped directly on a Christmas tree or suspended with a piece of ribbon or decorative cord. Clip a carving to the top of a gift bag or the bow on a present for a special treat. The clothespins make a functional and decorative way to display Christmas cards. Hang a piece of yarn or twine and attach the cards to the yarn with carved clothespins.

You can carve any design into the clothespins. I carve traditional Christmas images, such as Santa, but you can carve spring flowers or fall leaves onto the clothespins for year-round decorations.

To carve the clothespins, pop off the spring. Use your tools of choice to carve the design in the two straight pieces of wood. Finish the carvings with acrylic paint, oil paint, or stain. After the finish dries, reassemble the clothespins and touch up any marks made during the reassembly process.

materials & tools

MATERIALS:
- Wooden spring-type clothespin
- Acrylic paint or finish of choice

TOOLS:
- Carving knife or tools of choice
- Carving glove and thumb guard
- Paintbrush

Clothespins can be carved and painted as decorations for any season.

Easy Santa
Ornament

By Dan Haack

I designed this Santa ornament specifically for simplicity. I make a template out of thin plastic, such as a coffee container lid, to quickly transfer guidelines. I carve wooden stamps to make painting Santa's eyes a snap.

These jolly Santas always attract attention. Carve them from butternut or red cedar and finish them naturally to highlight the beautiful grain of the wood.

I finish most of my carvings with paint washes. But I have discovered that people like Christmas ornaments shiny, so I use full-strength paint.

EYE STAMPS

tips

Rather than painting the tiny eyes with a paintbrush, I carve wooden stamps for the iris and pupil. Carve one end of a ¼" by ¼" by 2" blank into a ⅛"-diameter cylinder for the iris. Carve the other end or a similar blank into a ³⁄₃₂"-diameter cylinder for the pupil. Dip the cylinders in the appropriate paint and touch it to the carving for quick and easy eyes.

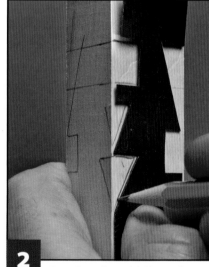

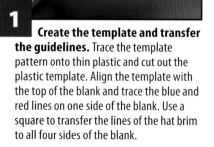

1 **Create the template and transfer the guidelines.** Trace the template pattern onto thin plastic and cut out the plastic template. Align the template with the top of the blank and trace the blue and red lines on one side of the blank. Use a square to transfer the lines of the hat brim to all four sides of the blank.

2 **Complete the guidelines.** Flip the template and trace the blue lines on the second side of the blank so the triangle of the nose meets at the corner of the blank. Trace the red lines on the third side of the blank so the square of the hat ball meets at the corner. Make an X on the top and bottom of the blank to keep the carving symmetrical.

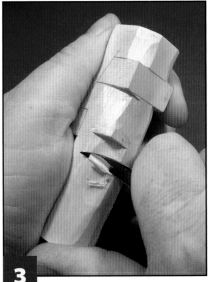

3 **Remove the sharp corners.** Make stop cuts under the tip of the nose and under the bottom of the hat brim above the nose. Carve up to the stop cuts to remove the triangular chips. Make a stop cut at the bottom of the ball on the hat and cut up to the stop cut to leave the ball raised. Round off all of the corners except the brim of the hat.

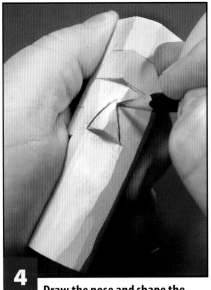

4 **Draw the nose and shape the hat tail.** Sketch in the triangle of the nose. Use the corner of the blank to keep the nose centered on the face. Carve the hat tail at a 45° angle toward the top center of the blank. The angled cut starts just above the brim of the hat.

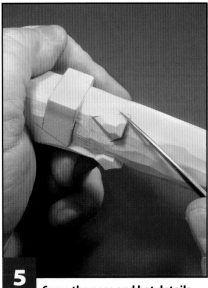

5 **Carve the nose and hat details.** Carve around the nose. Leave enough wood for the forehead and eyebrows. Carve off the bottom corners of the nose. Shape the hat tail and ball. Use a detail knife to lower the face. Leave wood for the cheeks, eyebrows, and the portion of the beard above the mustache.

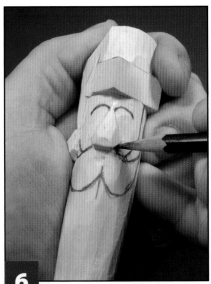

6 **Draw in the mustache.** Start the left side of the mustache at the bottom right corner of the hat ball. Draw in the matching right curve of the mustache that ends directly below the right corner of the hat brim. Draw the sides of the face, eyebrows, and bottom of the mustache, leaving room for the lip.

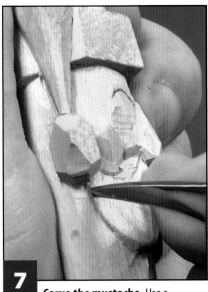

7 **Carve the mustache.** Use a detail knife to carve the bottom of the mustache and start shaping the bottom of the blank into the beard. Use the X on the bottom of the blank to maintain symmetry. Carve the sides of the face and shape the cheeks.

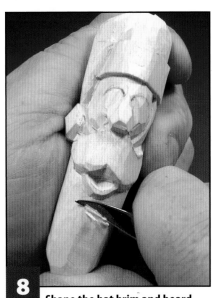

8 **Shape the hat brim and beard.** Round the hat brim. Carve in the bottom lip. The lip is lower than the mustache because the mustache covers the upper lip but stands proud of the beard. Round and shape the beard.

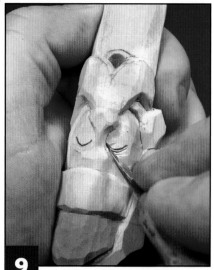

9 **Add facial details.** Round the bridge of the nose. Carve the eyebrows and round the forehead so it appears to be under the hat. Carve small triangles to represent simple nostrils. Refine the shape of the mustache. Draw in curved upper eyelids and carve them with a detail knife.

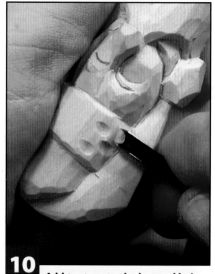

10 **Add texture to the hat and hair.** Carve small notches around the hat brim and hat ball with a ⅛" #11 gouge to make them appear fluffy. Use the same tool to carve grooves in the beard and upward swoops in the mustache.

11 **Carve the final details.** Remove the high points in the beard and mustache with a 1.5mm #9 gouge. Then remove the high points left from the #9 gouge with a 1mm 45° V-tool. Deepen some of the gouge grooves with the V-tool. Remove any chips with a stiff brush.

Ornament template

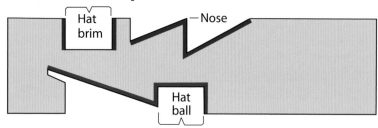

Santa ornament pattern

Photocopy at 100%

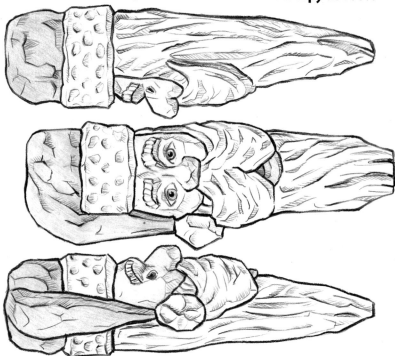

Painting the Carving

Apply an antique white base coat to the entire carving. Paint the hat brim, hat ball, and eyes white. Paint the exposed skin with Santa flesh. Paint the hat bright red. Paint the eyes blue and add black pupils; use the eye stamps described on page 12 if you wish. Add white highlights to the eyes with a toothpick. Add a small eye hook, apply a coat of wax, and buff to a nice shine.

materials & tools

MATERIALS:	TOOLS:
• 1" x 1" x 4" basswood or wood of choice	• Rough out knife
• Acrylic paints:	• Detail knife
Antique white	• 1.5mm #9 gouge
White	• ⅛" #11 gouge
Bright red	• 1mm 45° V-tool
Santa flesh	• Stiff vegetable or denture brush
Black	• Soft buffing brush
Blue	• Assorted paintbrushes
• Paste wax	• Small square
• Stiff plastic (template)	• Eye stamps

Create a Playful Chris-Moose Ornament

By Cyndi Joslyn

Take a break from Santa with a humorous Christmas moose ornament. The individual parts are easy to carve and assembly is simple. Chris-Moose (Chris for short) will hang on just about anything. He is designed to hang out on the Christmas tree, but my family takes turns hanging Chris all around the house. He's been spotted clinging to a bed frame, a mirror, and even a cupboard door!

Use the patterns as a guide to carve the parts of the moose. Don't be too concerned with accuracy. As long as it looks somewhat like a moose, people will love it.

Chris-moose ornament pattern

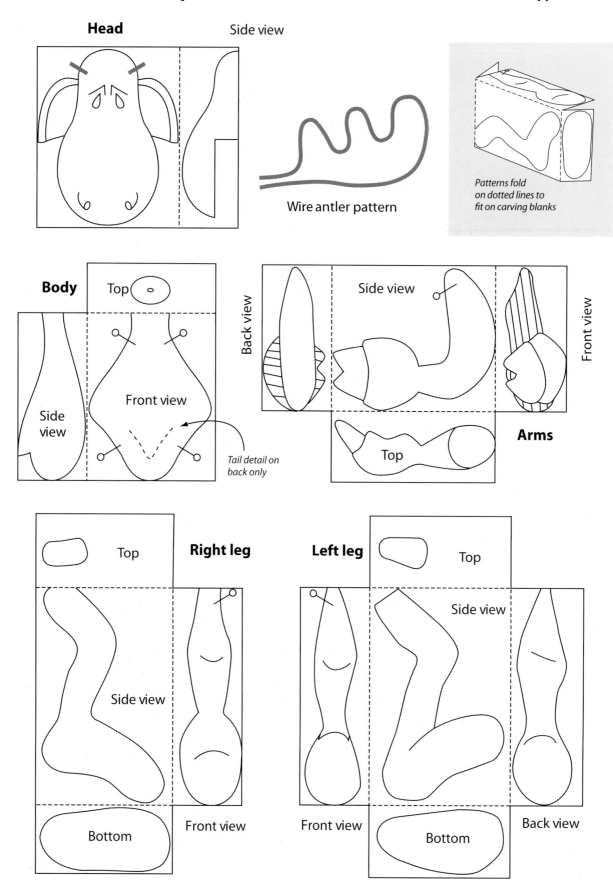

Head

Side view

Wire antler pattern

Patterns fold on dotted lines to fit on carving blanks

Body

Top

Side view

Front view

Tail detail on back only

Back view

Side view

Front view

Top

Arms

Top

Right leg

Side view

Bottom

Front view

Left leg

Top

Side view

Front view

Bottom

Back view

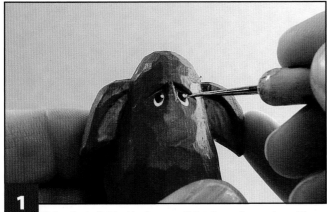

1 Paint the individual body parts. Paint the entire carving with a mixture of equal parts of burnt sienna and spice brown. Apply two coats. Apply dark flesh to the inside of the ears. Use a liner brush to add slanted ovals of light ivory for the whites of the eyes. Let the paint dry and add the black pupil with a liner brush. Apply a light ivory highlight dot to the right upper corner of the eyes with a stylus.

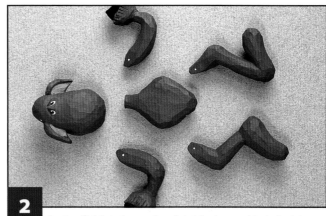

2 Apply a finish to the carving. Paint the hooves black. Seal the carving with a mixture of equal parts water-based varnish and water and allow it to dry. Mix one part raw sienna with one part burnt sienna and two parts retarder medium. Apply the mixture to the carving with a brush and immediately wipe off most of the mixture with a soft rag. The antiquing mixture imparts an aged look to the carving.

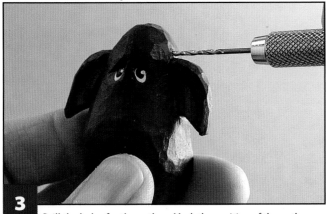

3 Drill the holes for the antlers. Mark the position of the antlers above each ear using the pattern as a guide. Drill ¹⁄₁₆"-diameter holes ¼" deep with a manual drill.

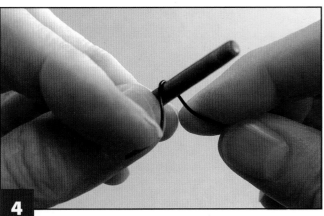

4 Create the antlers. Use the antler pattern as a guide to bend the wire to shape. Wrap the wire around the end of a paintbrush to shape the antlers. Create two identical antlers. String two jingle bells on each antler.

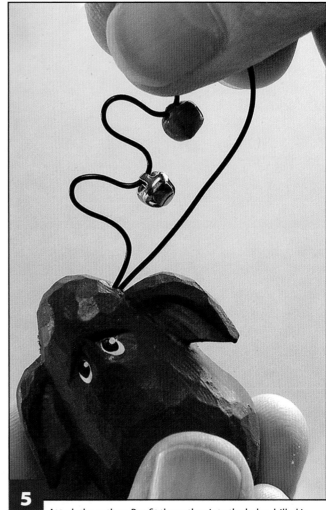

5 Attach the antlers. Dry fit the antlers into the holes drilled in the moose's head. When you are happy with the placement, glue the antlers in place with cyanoacrylate (CA) glue. Use a drop of CA glue to hold the bells in place as well.

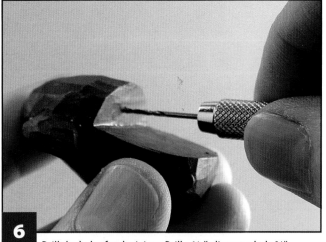

6 Drill the holes for the joints. Drill a ¹⁄₁₆"-diameter hole ³⁄₈" deep on the back of the head and on the top of the body with a manual drill. Drill ¼"-deep holes on the body where the arms and legs will be attached. Then drill the holes in the arms and legs. Do not drill the whole way through the arms or legs.

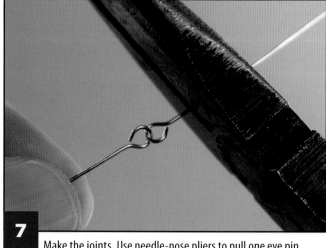

7 Make the joints. Use needle-nose pliers to pull one eye pin slightly apart. Hook the open eye pin through another eye pin. Use the needle-nose pliers to close the eye pin. Make five joint sets. Trim the posts on four joint sets to ¼" long. Trim the posts on the fifth set to ³⁄₈" long.

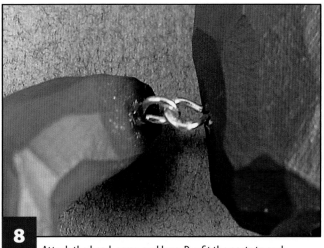

8 Attach the head, arms, and legs. Dry fit the posts to each hole to make sure the hole is deep enough. The head of the eye pin should be flush with the carving. Use the pin with the ³⁄₈"-long posts to attach the head to the body. Use CA glue to secure all of the posts to the carving, assembling the moose.

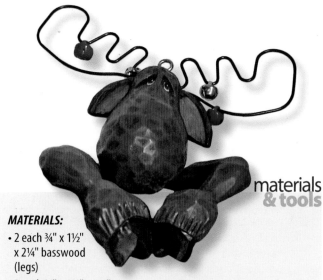

materials & tools

MATERIALS:
- 2 each ¾" x 1½" x 2¼" basswood (legs)
- 2 each ¾" x 1½" x 1½" basswood (arms)
- ¾" x 1⅜" x 1¾" basswood (body)
- ⅝" x 1½" x 1⅞" basswood (head)
- 2 each 7" length of 20-gauge, black-coated wire (antlers)
- 10 each eye pins (found in jewelry section of craft store)
- 4 each ¼"-diameter jingle bells
- Acrylic paint:
  Burnt sienna
  Spice brown
  Black
  Light ivory
  Dark flesh
  Raw sienna
- Satin interior varnish
- Acrylic retarder medium
- Soft cloth, such as old T-shirt, for antiquing
- Cyanoacrylate glue

TOOLS:
- ⅝" #3 gouge
- Bench knife
- Detail knife
- 1mm V-tool
- Manual drill (pin vise) with ¹⁄₁₆"-diameter bit
- Needle-nose pliers
- #6 flat brush
- #1 liner brush

Easy Evergreen Puzzle

By Sandy Smith

This quick and easy evergreen tree combines a fun puzzle with a folk-style Christmas ornament. They make wonderful gifts and always prompt smiles.

To get started, make a template from clear, flexible plastic such as a coffee can lid. Trace the pattern, including the centerline, shoulder, and hip, onto the template with a permanent marker. Cut the template out with scissors. Be sure to wear your carving glove when carving the small pieces.

To present the puzzle as a gift, wrap the separated pieces in tissue paper and place them in a gift bag with a photo of the assembled puzzle. Include an instruction sheet noting that each piece must be assembled in a specific order, starting at the bottom and working up to the top, then putting the chain through the hole to secure the puzzle.

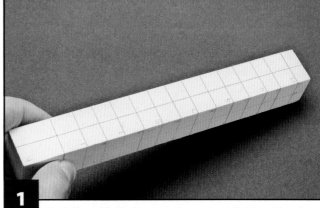

1 **Mark the grid.** Mark a centerline on two adjoining sides of the blank. Label the left and right sides L and R. Measure down 1" from the top, and draw a horizontal line across the two sides. Mark horizontal lines in ½" increments the rest of the way to the end. Starting at the horizontal line 1½" from the top, number the lines—odd numbers on the right side, even on the left.

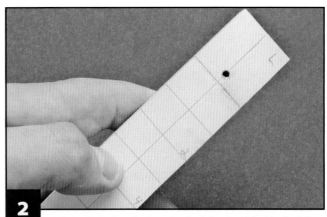

2 **Drill the hole for the key.** On the left side of the blank, drill a ⅛"-diameter hole all the way through the blank about ⅛" above the first line along the centerline (⅞" from the top). This hole is for the chain that will hold the puzzle together and be used to hang the ornament. It is easier to drill this hole now while the blank is still square.

MARKING THE PIECES   **tips**

Permanently mark each piece so you can easily reassemble it if the pieces should happen to get mixed together. Marking them with dots—think dominoes—is a simple way to distinguish their proper order. Label each piece in the center of the socket— it's hidden when the puzzle is assembled, but obvious to those who have no patience for puzzles.

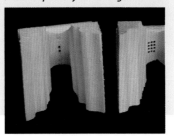

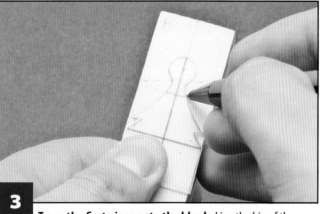

3 **Trace the first piece onto the blank.** Line the hip of the template up with line 1 on the R side. Align the centerlines of the template and the blank. Trace around the template. The tops (knob and neck) of all of the pieces will be similar. The section between the shoulder and the hip should vary from piece to piece.

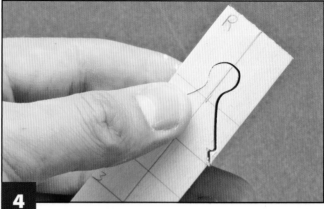

4 **Cut the first puzzle piece.** Use a scroll saw and a #3 reverse skip-tooth blade. Begin and end on the hip line. Vary the cut by adding bumps and dips between the shoulder and the hip. By varying the shape, you ensure each piece has a specific place in the puzzle. Remove the first piece, label it A, and set it aside.

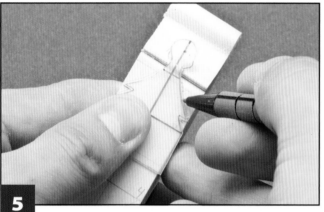

5 **Cut the second puzzle piece.** Using the template, line the hip up with line 2 on the L side. Trace around the template as you did in step 3. Cut the second puzzle piece, starting and ending at the hip line. Remove the second piece, label it B, and set it aside.

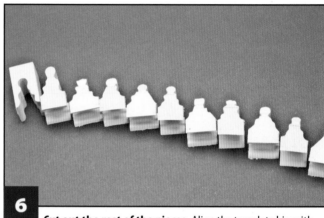

6 **Cut out the rest of the pieces.** Align the template hip with line 3 on the R side, and trace around the template. Cut piece C. Remember to customize each piece between the shoulder and hip. Draw each piece just before you cut it, until all the pieces are cut.

7 **Shape the top piece.** On the square portion of the top piece, draw diagonal lines from corner to corner to find the center. Carve up to the center mark, shaping this piece into the top of the tree. Carve off the sharp lower edges from the center out to the scrolled edges to round the piece.

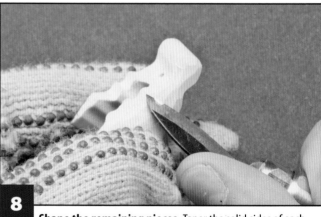

8 **Shape the remaining pieces.** Taper the solid sides of each piece from the hip to the knob to form a pyramid shape. Remove ¼" from each side, leaving the knob ½" wide. Do not alter the perimeter from the knob to the hip where it fits into the adjoining piece. You are only reducing the width—not altering the shape.

9 **Texture the pieces.** Cut from the bottom of the piece toward the tip and center to create the look of branches. Use both a large and small veiner and vary the depth and width of the gouge marks for a natural look. Round the corners and the cut edges not associated with the puzzle connection areas. Smooth and round the last piece to simulate the trunk of a tree.

10 **Make the oil stain.** Mix equal parts of boiled linseed oil (BLO) and mineral spirits in a jar. Add two parts green oil paint and one part blue oil paint to the BLO/mineral spirits mixture. I mix ½ cup BLO, ½ cup mineral spirits, 1 teaspoon green oil paint, and ½ teaspoon blue oil paint. Mix or shake the jar until the paint pigment dissolves in the BLO/mineral spirits mixture.

11 **Stain the pieces.** Add the pieces to the jar, and move them around with a stick for at least a minute. Make sure they are well-coated and blue-green in color. Remove the pieces and drain them on paper towels. Dab off any excess oil and set them aside to dry. BLO soaked towels can spontaneously combust. Be sure to dispose of the oily paper towels in a safe manner.

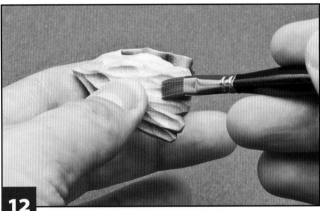

12 **Apply the final finishes to the pieces.** Use a stiff-bristled brush to dry-brush the edges and high ridges with white acrylic paint. Paint the lower edges with acrylic iridescent pearl glitter paint. Paint the trunk with a thick wash of raw umber acrylic paint. Wax each individual piece with neutral shoe polish. Buff each piece to a lustrous glow. Assemble the puzzle and chain.

materials & tools

MATERIALS:
- 1" x 1" x 8" basswood (or wood of your choice)
- 6" pull chain with a connector (found at hardware stores)
- Jingle bell (for chain, optional)
- Clear plastic lid (for template)
- Boiled linseed oil
- Mineral spirits
- Oil paints:
  Blue
  Green
- Acrylic paints:
  White
  Raw umber
  Iridescent pearl glitter
- Neutral shoe polish
- Paper towels
- Disposable rubber gloves

TOOLS:
- Pencil
- Ruler
- Scissors
- Drill with ⅛"-diameter drill bit
- Scroll saw with #3 reverse skip-tooth blade
- Carving knife
- Veiner: 6mm, 3mm
- Stiff-bristle paintbrush
- Soft-bristle paintbrush (to add the pearl glitter paint)
- Small jar (to mix the BLO, mineral spirits, and oil paint)
- Shoe buffing brush

Tree puzzle template

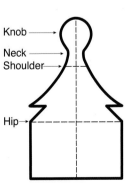

Knob →
Neck →
Shoulder →
Hip →

Photocopy at 100%

Carving a Star Ornament

By Jim Sebring
Step-by-step photos by Jody Sebring

Dress up your Christmas tree with handcarved stars! The stars are ideal for highlighting garlands or wreaths and make perfect stocking stuffers.

Carve the stars from a solid piece of basswood or butternut. To add interest, create laminated blanks by gluing together several thin pieces of colorful hardwood. The contrasting layers will be exposed as you carve the star.

I use a reciprocating carver for hardwood stars, securing the blank in a homemade jig and using a ¾" straight chisel. If you are carving laminated stars without a reciprocating carver, use softer woods such as cedar, basswood, or butternut, which are easier to carve.

Use spray adhesive to attach the paper pattern to a piece of stiff plastic (from a blister pack or something similar) to make a template. Cut the template carefully with a hobby knife and a straight edge to keep the size and angles accurate. Cut out the center so you can mark the chip carving lines on the blank.

Securely clamp hardwood stars in a vertical position before carving the points. If you're using soft wood you can hold it in your hand to carve, but be sure to wear a carving glove.

I carve hundreds of stars each year and developed a holding fixture to speed production. Patterns for creating the custom holding jig are on page 25, and instructions are available here:
www.woodcarvingillustrated.com/tools-and-tips/star-carving-fixture.html.

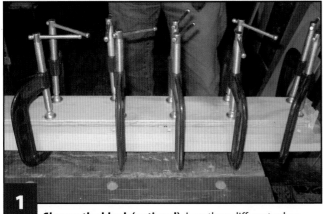

1 **Glue up the blank (optional).** I use three different colors of wood. Sandwich the center layer between two matching pieces of wood. Then use a third color of wood for the outermost layers. Make sure the grain runs the same direction on all of the pieces. Spread yellow wood glue on both of the sides to be glued together and clamp the layers together overnight.

2 **Transfer the pattern to the blank.** Use a square to mark lines perpendicular to the direction of the grain. Make sure the top point of the star (marked with an X) runs with the grain of the wood. The grain runs from the point with the X toward the bottom of the star. Trace around the perimeter pattern with a pencil.

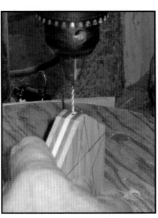

3 **Cut the blank.** Cut the V-shape from between the bottom two points. Cutting straight across the bottom points provides a flat surface to support the star during drilling. Use a #56 drill bit and drill a hole in the center of the top point for the hanger loop. Cut the remainder of the star outline.

4 **Trace the center star.** Align the X point on the pattern with the X point on the blank. Trace the center star design on to the blank. Flip the blank. Keep the template face up, align the X points, and trace the center design on the back of the blank.

5 **Carve the center.** Use a bench knife or chip carving knife. Make angled cuts from the lines down to the center. It may take several cuts. The cuts converge at the center of the star, which should end up about ¼" deep. Carve the center on both sides. Then draw a centerline around the perimeter of the blank.

6 **Make the stop cuts.** Securely clamp the star and use a small hobby saw. Make a stop cut at each intersection of the star's points. Angle the stop cut from the centerline along the perimeter of the star to the edge of the chip-carved design in the center. Make the cuts on both sides of the star.

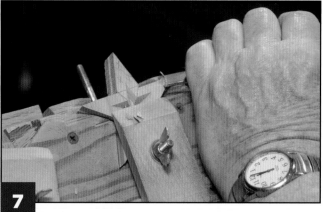

7 **Begin carving the points.** Follow the suggested cut order and direction to avoid breaking off the points. Clamp the star and use a reciprocating carver or mallet and chisel for hardwood stars. Use a knife for soft wood stars. Hold the blade at an angle so the center of the point is highest. Make cuts 1, 2, and 3.

8 **Finish carving the points.** Flip the blank over and repeat cuts 1, 2, and 3 on the reverse side. Continue making the cuts in the order and direction shown below. Turn and flip the star as required. Some of the cuts may feel awkward, but it is the best progression to avoid breaking the points.

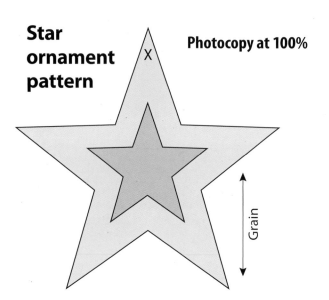

9 **Finish the stars.** Sand the flat planes of the points with a piece of sandpaper glued to a flat piece of wood. Glue the hanger loop in place with cyanoacrylate (CA) glue. Apply two light coats of lacquer, sanding lightly between coats.

materials & tools

MATERIALS:
- 5 each ⅛" x 3" x 3" contrasting colors of wood (laminated star)
- ⅝" x 3" x 3" basswood, cedar, or butternut (solid star)
- Lacquer or finish of choice
- Yellow wood glue
- Eye hanger
- Sandpaper, 220 grit
- Cyanoacrylate glue

TOOLS:
- Chip carving knife or knife of choice
- Straight chisel and mallet or reciprocating power carver with straight chisel attachment (hardwood star)
- Saw of choice (to cut blanks)
- Hobby saw (to make stop cuts)
- Safety glove
- Drill with #56 twist bit

Star ornament pattern

Photocopy at 100%

Grain

Progression of cuts for hand carving

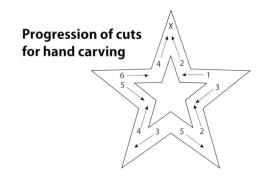

Progression of cuts for power carving

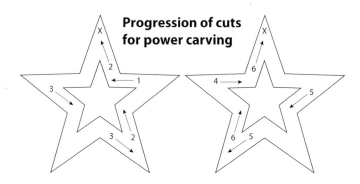

Star ornament jig pattern

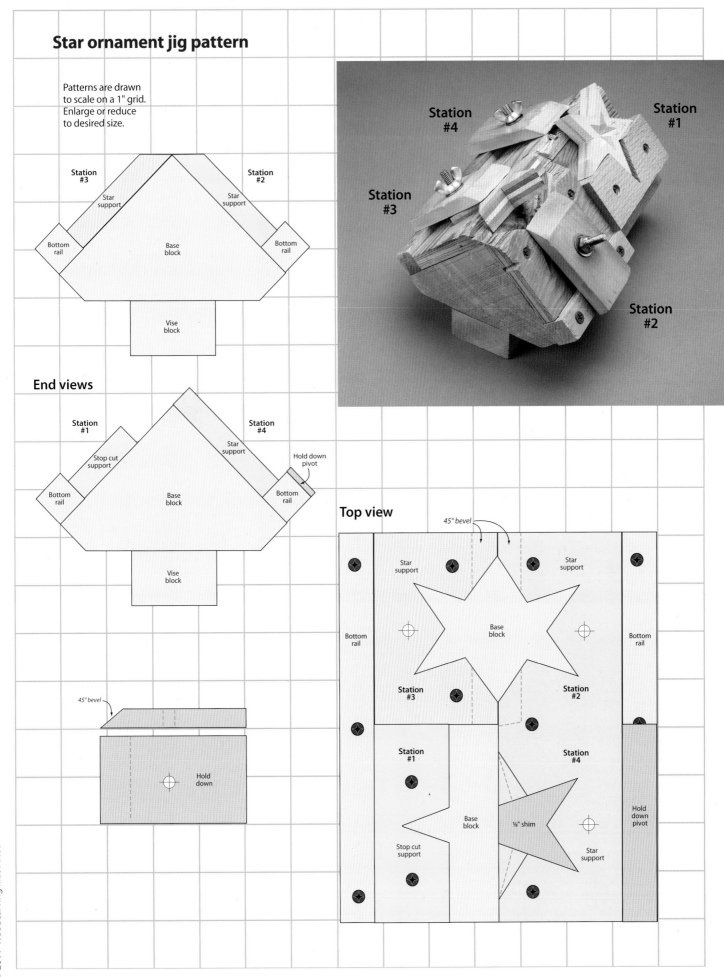

Patterns are drawn to scale on a 1" grid. Enlarge or reduce to desired size.

Station #3

Station #2

Star support

Star support

Bottom rail

Base block

Bottom rail

Vise block

End views

Station #1

Station #4

Stop cut support

Star support

Hold down pivot

Bottom rail

Base block

Bottom rail

Vise block

45° bevel

Hold down

Station #4

Station #1

Station #3

Station #2

Top view

45° bevel

Star support

Star support

Bottom rail

Base block

Bottom rail

Station #3

Station #2

Station #1

Station #4

Base block

⅛" shim

Star support

Stop cut support

Hold down pivot

© 2011 Woodcarving Illustrated

Hangin' On Santa Ornament

By Steve Brown

This whimsical fellow can be carved quickly for a great holiday gift. Designed as a decorative fan pull, it also makes a great Christmas tree ornament.

The candy cane is made from lead-free plumber's soldering wire. Drill a hole the same size as the wire in the hand and glue the candy cane in place. The soldering wire looks thick, but it is easy to bend and shape. If you are making a fan pull, drill a ⅛"-diameter hole in the hand for the fan pull chain.

Thin acrylic paint with water to the consistency of a wash for the Santa and use undiluted white and red enamel paint for the candy cane.

Hangin' On Santa patterns

Photocopy at 100%

MATERIALS:

- 1½" x 2" x 5" basswood
- Acrylic paints:
  Maroon (coat, pants, and high-lights on cheeks and nose)
  Dark forest (gloves)
  Burnt umber (boots)
  Antique white (beard, moustache, and hair)
  White (fur)
  Medium flesh (face)
- Enamel paints:
  White (candy cane)
  Red (candy cane)
- 6" piece of lead-free plumber's soldering wire (candy cane)
- Pull chain cord and connector

TOOLS:

- Palm-size V-tools: ¹⁄₁₆", ⅛", ⁵⁄₁₆"
- ³⁄₁₆" palm-size veiner
- ³⁄₁₆" #9 gouge
- Carving knife
- Carving glove
- Drill
- ⅛"-diameter drill bit
- Drill bit the same diameter as plumber's soldering wire
- Paintbrushes of choice

SPECIAL SOURCES:
Santa Fan Pull roughouts are available from *www.sbrownwoodcarving.com*, or 270-821-8774.

© 2011 Woodcarving Illustrated

Relief Carve Santa Ornaments

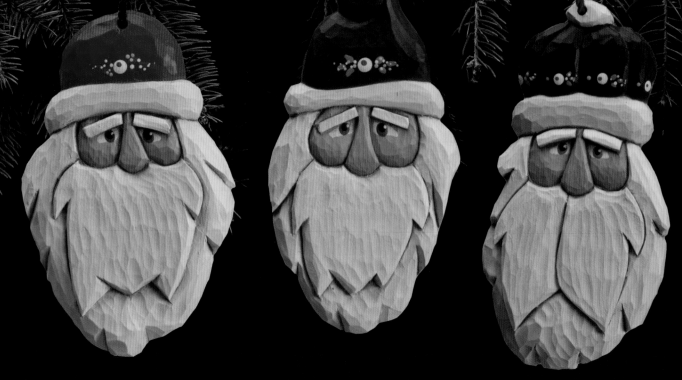

By Cyndi Joslyn

These relief-carved ornaments require only simple cuts with little to no undercutting. You can customize the different designs by changing the hat color.

Transfer the pattern to the ⅜"-thick basswood and cut the perimeter of the ornaments with a band saw or scroll saw. Drill ⅛"-diameter holes in the tops for the hanging strings. I remove the saw marks and add texture to the beard and mustache right away so I can tuck an ornament and knife in my bag to carve when I have spare time.

I paint the ornaments assembly-line style. Paint the white triangles for the eyes. When dry, add a dot for the iris. A black dot at the top of the iris forms the pupil and a white highlight dot is added on top of the pupil. Allow the dots to dry thoroughly before adding the next color. When dry, seal the carving with water-based varnish and apply an antiquing medium and wipe off the excess with a paper towel.

materials & tools

MATERIALS:
- ⅜" x 2¾" x 3½ to 4½" basswood or wood of choice
- Acrylic paints:
  Light ivory (beard, whites of eyes)
  Medium flesh (face)
  Adobe (face blush)
  Ivory (fur trim)
  Western sunset (hat)
  Passion (hat)
  Tomato spice (hat)
  Blue velvet (hat)
  Hunter green (hat)
  Blue heaven (blue irises)
  Autumn brown (brown irises)
  Black (pupils)
- Water-based varnish
- Antiquing medium
- Hanging string

TOOLS:
- Scroll saw or band saw
- Detail knife
- ⅝" #3 palm gouge
- 6mm #7 palm gouge
- Carving glove
- Paintbrushes of choice
- Drill with ⅛"-diameter bit

Power Carving a Dove Ornament

By Hugh Parks

Create realistic feather details with a woodburner.

This dove ornament is an excellent way to practice texturing techniques. Because the ornament is essentially a relief carving, you can finish the project quickly. The carved dove makes a great gift or addition to your Christmas tree.

This ornament evolved from the annual Christmas ornament exchange between members of the *Woodcarving Illustrated* message board. Compared to some of the wonderfully carved ornaments I received, I felt my ornaments were little more than trinkets. I designed and carved this dove ornament as something credible to exchange with my carving buddies.

The dove is light enough to be used as a Christmas tree ornament or wreath embellishment. I use white cedar or tupelo wood. Trace the outline of the pattern onto a 1"-thick piece of wood. Avoid wood with knots and highly figured grain. Cut around the outline of the pattern on a band saw.

1 **Draw the major landmarks.** Use the pattern as a guide to draw the outline of the head, cheek, position of the eye, neck, and the outline of the rear wing onto the blank with an HB pencil. Sketch in the front wing on the back of the carving. Draw a centerline on the edges of the wings.

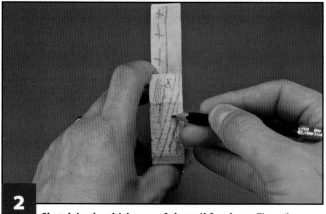

2 **Sketch in the thickness of the tail feathers.** The tail feathers are 1/16" thick on the completed carving. Draw a curved line on the edge of the tail. The line runs diagonally from the wings toward the breast and angles from the front of the bird toward the back. Move 1/16" and draw a line parallel to the first line.

3 **Rough carve the wings.** Use a large cylinder-shaped flat-end Typhoon bit to remove wood down to the centerline of the rear wing. Use the same bit to remove wood from the back of the front wing down to the centerline. Leave the pencil lines intact. Shape the tight corners with a small pointed Typhoon bit.

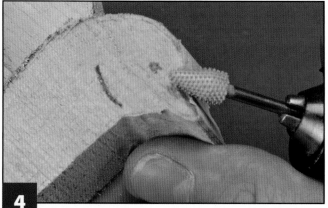

4 **Rough out the head.** Doves have small rounded heads. Carefully round the head and shape the area where the head intersects with the bill. Use a small pointed Typhoon bit and sand it smooth. Draw a centerline from the top of the head to the end of the bill and draw in the bill.

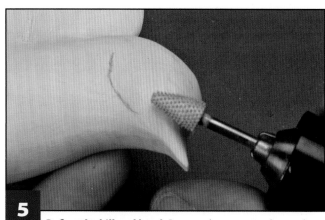

5 **Refine the bill and head.** Remove the extra wood around the bill with a small pointed Typhoon bit. Round the edges of the head with the same bit. You don't have a lot of wood to work with, so go slowly. Work down the neck, shaping it and creating a smooth transition.

6 **Shape the rump area.** Draw in the rump and tail area using the pattern as a guide. Remove wood from the top and bottom of the tail using a large cylinder-shaped flat-end Typhoon bit. The tail should slope downward as you move from left to right. Leave the pencil marks. Round the edges of the tail and give it a fan shape.

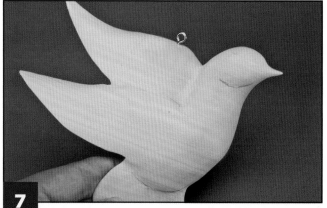

7 **Round the breast.** Work from the head down to the tail. Use a 1/2"-diameter cushioned sanding drum equipped with 80-grit Swiss sanding paper. Use the same tool to round the front of the wings and add a slight taper to the bottom of the wings. Bring the edges to a point at the tip of the wings.

8 **Hollow the back of the carving.** Use the same sanding drum. Run your fingers over the front of the carving while sanding. You can feel the vibration of the sanding drum in any thin spots. Use the tool at a slow speed so you don't catch the edge of the carving and break off a section of the wings or tail.

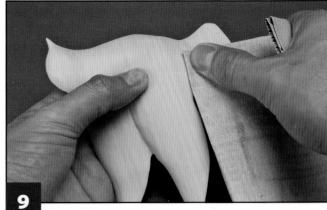

9 **Sand the dove.** Start with 80-grit sandpaper. Move on to 150 grit and then 220 grit. Use caution when sanding the bill. Spray the carving with denatured alcohol to raise the grain and sand it again with 220-grit or finer sandpaper. Sketch in the primary, secondary, and shoulder feathers.

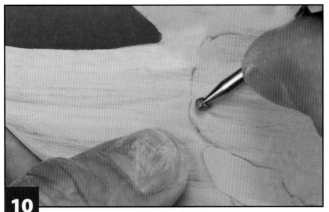

10 **Relieve along the feathers.** Use a ball-shaped diamond bit. Carve the primary, secondary, and shoulder feathers on both wings and the tail section. Sand the edges. Draw in the cheek line. Relieve along the line and add ripples to the cheek with the same bit. Blend the edges to make a smooth transition. Drill a 4mm eyehole the entire way through the carving.

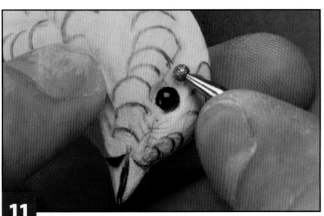

11 **Add the eye.** Add the eye channel, running from the rear of the bill just past the eyehole, with a ball-shaped diamond bit. Drill a 5mm hole up through the back of the 4mm hole with the same bit. Stop when the bulge of the ball protrudes through the front of the carving. Leave enough wood to hold the eye in place. Insert the eye through the back and fill the hole with two-part epoxy.

12 **Add texture to the feathers.** Draw in the feathers on the head and breast. Burn in the feather details with a skew woodburning pen or a use a cylinder-shaped stone to carve the texture. Seal the wood with your sealer of choice.

DOVE ORNAMENT: PAINTING NOTES

Mix white acrylic paint with a small amount of black and paint the entire carving to shade it a very light gray. Highlight the edge of each feather with two to three coats of straight white. The goal is to create a gray feather with a white edge. Thin white paint heavily with water or flow medium and apply several washes to the entire carving. Do not hide the gray centers of the feathers. Mix a little black into the original gray mixture and apply the mixture to the feather splits. Paint the bill black. Add a small black edge to some of the primary wing feathers. Add pearlescent or iridescent white to the quills and apply matte medium varnish to the quills and the bill. Attach a small eyelet to the top of the rear wing to hang the ornament.

materials & tools

MATERIALS:
- 1" x 5" x 6" tupelo or white cedar
- Assorted grits of Swiss sanding paper up to 220 grit
- Denatured alcohol
- Two-part epoxy
- 5mm brown eye
- Sealer
- Acrylic paints:
  White
  Black
  Pearlescent or iridescent white
- Matte medium varnish
- Eyelet

TOOLS:
- HB pencil
- Large cylinder-shaped flat-end Typhoon bit
- Small pointed Typhoon bit
- ½"-diameter cushioned sanding drum
- 4mm drill bit
- Ball-shaped diamond bit
- Woodburner with skew pen or cylinder-shaped stone

Dove ornament pattern

Photocopy at 100%

Carving

By Floyd Rhadigan

These ornaments are easy to carve and finish. Both require only a few tools and four colors of paint. Create them using an assembly-line style to quickly build an inventory for holiday gift giving.

Ornament-Top Santa

Orient the block of wood so the nose lines up with the corner of the blank. Using the corner of the block makes it easier to give the face a triangular shape. Sketch in guidelines for the hat, then rough-shape and round the ornament before carving any details. Carve the ornament using your tools of choice. Add the beard texture last.

Star-Beard Santa

This design was inspired by my friend and fellow Caricature Carvers of America member Bruce Henn. Cut out the blank with a band saw and draw a centerline from the top of the hat to the bottom of the beard. Use a knife to taper both sides

Caricature Santa Ornaments

down from the centerline, creating a gentle triangular shape. Sketch on the facial details and carve them using your tools of choice. After carving the face, draw the stars on the beard. Stop-cut around the perimeter of the stars and remove ⅛" of wood from inside the stars. Hollow out the back of the beard until you reach the star-shaped holes. Then add the texture to the beard.

Finishing the Ornaments

When the carving is complete, scrub the piece with a stiff denture brush, hot water, and dish soap. Rinse off the soap and allow the carving to dry. Seal the carving with matte finish. Thin your acrylic paints of choice with water and paint the carving. I add one drop of paint to 20 drops of water and mix it well. Use slightly thicker paint for the eyes. Allow the paint to dry and seal it with a second coat of matte finish. To antique the carving, apply a mixture of equal parts dark and natural finishing wax with a stiff-bristle brush. Wipe off the excess wax and buff the carving with paper towels. Add a screw eye to the top of the carving and attach a ribbon or string.

Ornament-Top Santa

Star-Beard Santa

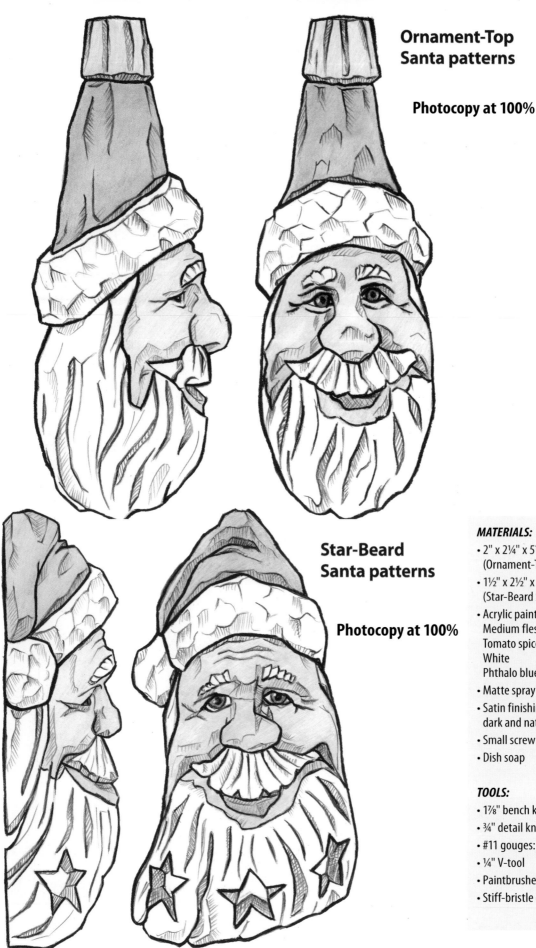

**Ornament-Top
Santa patterns**

Photocopy at 100%

**Star-Beard
Santa patterns**

Photocopy at 100%

materials
& tools

MATERIALS:
- 2" x 2¼" x 5½" basswood
  (Ornament-Top Santa)
- 1½" x 2½" x 4¾" basswood
  (Star-Beard Santa)
- Acrylic paint:
  Medium flesh
  Tomato spice
  White
  Phthalo blue
- Matte spray finish
- Satin finishing wax,
  dark and natural
- Small screw eyes
- Dish soap

TOOLS:
- 1⅞" bench knife
- ¾" detail knife
- #11 gouges: ¼", ³⁄₁₆", 3mm
- ¼" V-tool
- Paintbrushes of choice
- Stiff-bristle denture brush

Heirloom Santa Ornament

By Wayne Shinlever

I love the nostalgic look of classic tapered glass ornaments. This Santa ornament is modeled after those vintage designs, but is far more durable. It makes a delightful gift. Carve several and paint the "glass" in bright jewel tones to add Christmas cheer to your own tree.

1 **Cut the blank.** Trace the outline of the ornament on the front and side of the blank. Cut along the lines with a band saw. Shave off three of the sharp corners with a band saw table set to a 45° angle or use a sharp knife. Draw a circle on the top of the blank.

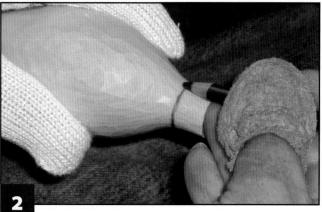

2 Round the blank. Carve a cylinder shape for the metal hanger. Round the blank with a carving knife. Draw the line marking the bottom of the hanger. Make a shallow stop cut around the line and gently relieve the area below the hanger. Sketch in the face area.

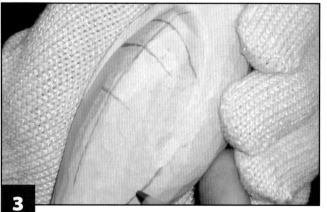

3 Begin shaping the face. Carve along the top and sides of the face with a 11mm #11 veiner. Draw a vertical centerline. Draw horizontal lines for the bottom of the hat, the eyes, and the base of the nose. Sketch in the beard. Cut across the eye mark with the same veiner. Make a stop cut along the hat line and taper the face up to the hat line.

4 Carve the eye sockets. Redraw the centerline and make a mark on either side of the line to establish the width of the bridge of the nose. The bridge of the nose is equal to the width of one eye. Use an 11mm #11 veiner to carve the eye sockets. Start at the side of the face and carve up to the bridge of the nose.

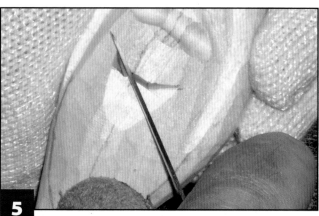

5 Rough out the nose. Make a stop cut along the bottom of the nose with a knife. Cut up to the stop cut from below to separate the nose from the lips and chin. Make stop cuts along the wings of the nose and cut up to the stop cuts from below.

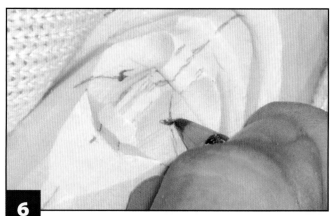

6 Determine the position of the nostrils. Make a horizontal line across the bridge of the nose half way between the brow and the tip of the nose. Make angled lines from the wings of the nose up to the horizontal line. Make a cross mark halfway along the angled lines.

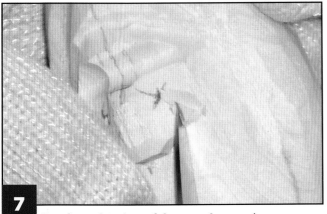

7 **Rough out the wings of the nose.** Cut up to the cross marks with a ¼" 60° V-tool to establish the top of the wings of the nose. Make stop cuts at the base of the V-tool cuts and cut up to the stop cuts from the side to establish the sides of the wings.

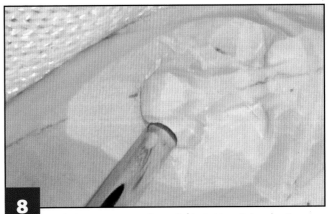

8 **Finish the nose.** Cut alongside the bridge of the nose from the wings up to the eyebrows with a 11mm #11 veiner. Round the tip and wings of the nose. Make stop cuts with a ¼" #9 gouge for the nostrils. Cut up to the stop cuts with the same gouge.

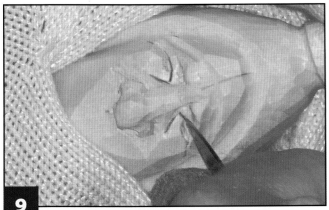

9 **Begin carving the eyes.** Draw a straight line across the eyes to keep them symmetrical. Cut a C-shape on the inside corner of each eye with an 11mm #2 gouge. Draw a small arch across the top of the straight line and make a stop cut straight in along the arched line.

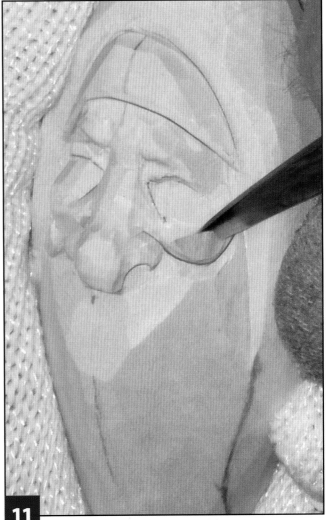

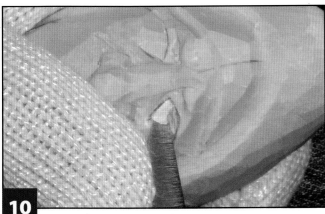

10 **Finish carving the eye.** Use a carving knife. Cut a wedge from the inside corner of the eyes. Carve upward across the eye to form the upper eyelid. Cut thin slits across the eyeballs to separate the upper and lower eyelids and produce a squinting effect.

11 **Carve the cheeks.** Draw hook shapes from the wings of the nose out to the edge of the face. Carve along the line with a ¼" 60° V-tool. Make a stop cut along the V-cut and cut down to the stop cut to form the bottom of the cheeks.

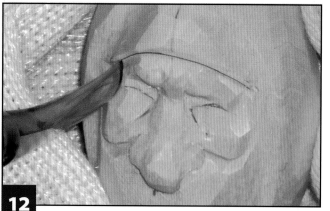

12 **Carve the temples.** Cut straight in at the temples with a ¾" #9 gouge. Then cut up to the stop cuts to free the chips and separate the temples from the "glass" area of the ornament.

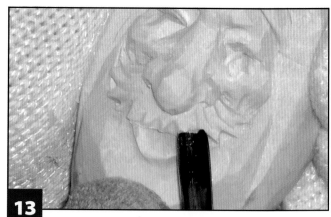

13 **Carve the mouth and mustache.** Draw in the mustache and cut along the line with a ¼" 60° V-tool. Undercut the mustache with a knife. Draw in the mouth and carve it with a knife. Use a 5mm #11 veiner to cut under the lower lip. Carve the mustache hair with a ¼" 60° V-tool.

14 **Carve the flowing beard.** Draw in the beard and carve along the lines with a 5mm #11 veiner. Separate the mustache from the beard by placing the veiner on its side and carving wood away from the beard. Carve the beard details with a ¼" #9 gouge. Add more texture to the beard with a 5mm #11 veiner.

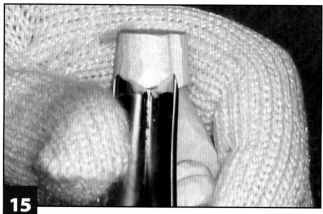

15 **Finish the carving.** Use a small V-tool to further texture the beard and add texture to the eyebrows. Use the same V-tool to carve the crow's feet and wrinkles under the eyes. Use a ¼" #11 veiner to add the grooves to the top of the metal hanger.

Painting the Ornament

Paint the hanger with full-strength gold patio paint. Paint the "glass" with red metallic paint. When it is dry, dip the piece in a bucket of pure boiled-linseed oil. Let the ornament drain for about ten minutes, then blot off any oil that pools in the deep cuts. Do not wipe the carving.

Dilute the rest of the colors with 15 to 20 drops of water for every drop of paint. Use medium flesh for the exposed flesh. Use a brush to add thinned tomato spice blush on the nose, cheeks, forehead, and upper eyelid to create the blush. If the blush is too strong, remove some of the color with a clean wet brush. Use adobe for the lip and antique white for the fur trim of the hat. The beard and mustache are painted with wicker white.

Create a lighter wash of burnt umber paint by adding a few extra drops of water. Use this mixture to paint the eyes and shade the deep crevices. Let the paint dry for about 20 minutes, then seal the carving with several coats of clear matte finish.

materials & tools

MATERIALS:
- 2½" x 2½" x 6¼" basswood
- Pure boiled linseed oil
- Acrylic paints:
  Gold patio paint
  Red metallic
  Medium flesh
  Tomato spice
  Adobe
  Antique white
  Wicker white
  Burnt umber
- Clear matte spray finish

TOOLS:
- Band saw
- Carving knife of choice
- 11mm #11 veiner
- ¼" 60° V-tool
- Small V-tool
- #9 gouges: ¼", ¾"
- ¼" #11 veiner
- 5mm #11 veiner
- 11mm #2 gouge
- Assorted paintbrushes

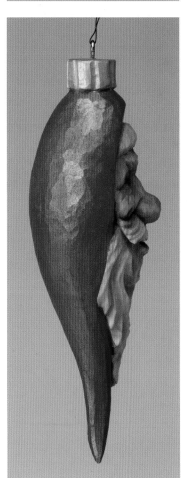

Heirloom ornament pattern

Olde World

By Mark Gargac

This olde world Santa demonstrates two styles of carving. Traditional relief carving techniques create the face and hat, but pierced relief adds texture and interest to the beard. Creating negative space or pierced cuts in the beard adds dimension and lends a nice flow to the carving.

Hollowing out the back of the ornament makes it lighter and easier to hang. The small size of the project cuts down on the investment of time and is a great way to build your confidence in creating realistic facial features before tackling more involved carvings. I suggest carving several ornaments and changing the expression or features on each.

These ornaments not only help build your carving skills, they also make great holiday gifts. Handcrafted gifts hold much more sentimental value than their store-bought counterparts. They're sure to become family heirlooms.

Always wear a carving glove for safety and take your time when hollowing the back; one slip can ruin your carving.

Santa Ornament

Variations

Even though the basic form of the carving remains the same, a few simple changes give Santa a whole new look. Try changing the position and shape of the nose. Turn the corners of the mustache up for a jolly look, or down for a more wizardly appearance. Change the shape of Santa's eyes for a quick and easy mood change. Changing Santa's hat is another way to make each carving unique.

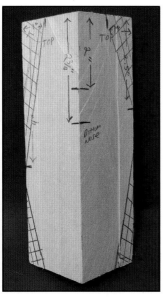

1 **Cut out the blank.** On a table saw or band saw, rip the blank lengthwise at a 45° angle to form two triangular pieces. For safety, rip a 21" blank, then cut it into 7" sections. Mark the landmarks of the carving. On the front corner, measure down 2" for the bottom of the hat and 2¾" for the nose. The tassel is 4" down on the left side of the blank. The bottom of the hat is 2½" down on the right side. At the top of the blank, the hat is 1" in from either side and tapers down to the first mark on that side. The shape of the beard can vary. Shade the areas to be removed.

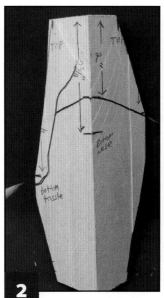

2 **Rough out the blank.** Carve away the shaded areas marked in step 1. Make a stop cut at the bottom of the hat with a detail knife, and taper up to the stop cut from ¼" down. Deepen the stop cut along the bottom of the hat at the front corner. Rough out the nose by cutting from the line marking the bottom of the nose up to the stop cut of the hat. Taper the hat from the bottom toward the top, but leave extra wood for the tassel. Use the front corner of the blank as a guide to draw a vertical centerline down the center of the nose.

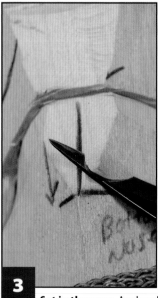
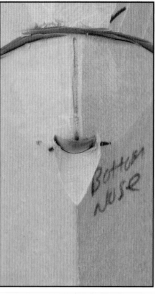
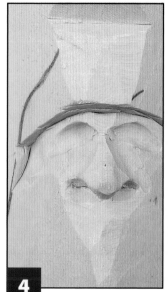
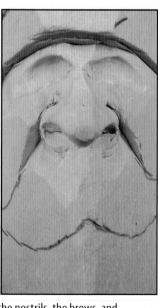

3

Set in the nose. Angle a detail knife and cut alongside the centerline from the bottom of the nose to the bottom of the hat. This removes the hard lines and elevates the nose from the face. Re-draw the centerline if you carved it away. Make stop cuts where the temple, bottom of the hat, and the tassel intersect. Cut the chip free. Invert a 5/16" #6 gouge and hold it at a slight angle to make a stop cut at the bottom of the nose. Flip the gouge over and cut from the chin up to the stop cut.

4

Block out the face. Shape the nostrils, the brows, and the forehead with a 5/16" #6 gouge. With this gouge, carve up alongside the nose to the eye sockets, and cut from the side of the face toward the eye socket to free the chip. Remove the sharp edges at the top of the mustache and make a V-shaped cut along the smile lines with a detail knife. Use a 3/16" #11 veiner to add depth to the eye sockets. Pencil in the mustache. Stop-cut along the bottom of the mustache, and taper up to it with a detail knife.

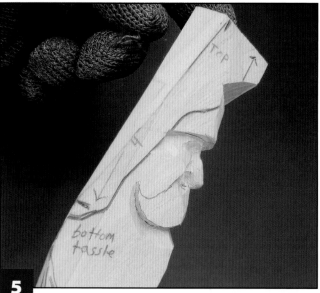

5

Rough out the sides and back. Remove a wedge of wood starting about 2¼" down from the top of the mustache to add depth and dimension to the beard. Shape the sides of the beard with a knife or a 13/16" #6 gouge. I mark the areas to remove with a cross hatch. You are simultaneously removing wood from the sides and back. Use the same gouge to hollow out the back of the beard. This makes the back of the beard concave and the front of the ornament convex. Leave the wood at least ¼" thick.

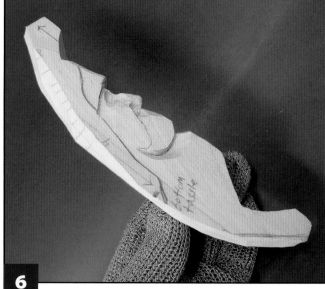

6

Finish shaping the hat. Remove wood from behind the top of the hat so it stands out (similar to the tip of the beard). Use a detail knife or a 13/16" #6 gouge. Carve from both the side and the back to "push" this area forward. You are removing the upper corners of the blank from the back. After you have rough-shaped the hat, use the same gouge to hollow the back of the hat. Leave the wood at least ¼"-thick. Sketch in the line for the tassel and make a V-shaped cut along the line with a detail knife.

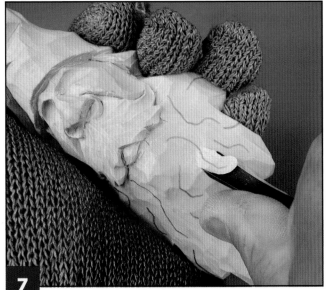

7 Shape the beard and mustache. Give the beard a smooth, flowing shape. Make a stop cut and taper the wood toward the top of the mustache. Separate the mustache with a ⅛" #11 veiner. Shape the lips. Use the veiner to rough texture the beard and mustache. Make triangular cuts around the edges of the beard with a detail knife. Pencil in random curved lines to break up the plane of the beard. Follow along these lines with a ⅜" #8 gouge.

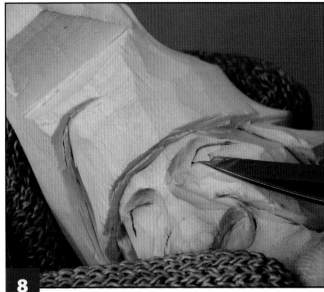

8 Carve the upper eyes. Sketch an arched line where the eye meets the upper eyelid. Make a deep stop cut slightly above the pencil line and cut up to the stop cut from below with a detail knife. You want the cut to be deep enough to be shadowed. Don't be afraid to repeat the step to make the stop cut deeper. Make sure the cuts for both eyes are the same. Another option is to make this cut the whole way through to the hollowed back.

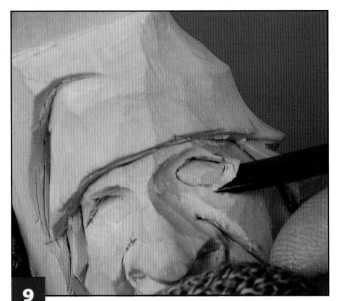

9 Carve the bags below the eyes. Invert a ¼" #6 gouge and press it in at a downward angle from the eye to make a stop cut. The corner of the gouge should meet the cut made on the outside of the upper eyelid. Keep one corner of the gouge in the wood, and slide the tool up to extend the cut to the inside corner of the eye. Flip the gouge right side up, and cut the chip free using the same sliding technique. Repeat the step for the opposite eye. This is one area where you can personalize your carving by changing the shape and depth of these cuts.

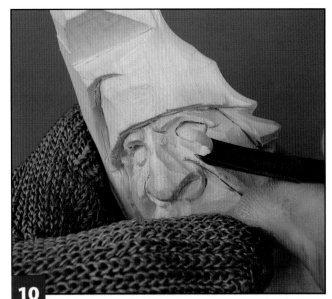

10 Add the secondary smile line. This detail really adds character to your carving. Using a 3⁄16" #11 veiner, cut from the hollow of the face below the cheekbones up between the eye and bridge of the nose. Use the smile line as a guide, but do not cut too close to it. If you cut too close, it may cut off the ridge that defines the primary smile line. Once that ridge is gone, it is difficult to carve another one and maintain the proper proportions. Take light cuts and make sure the corners of the veiner do not drop below the surface of the wood.

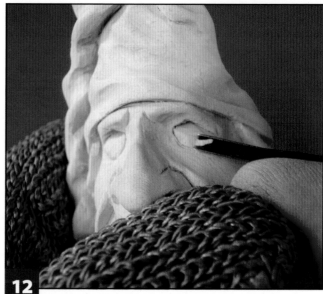

11 **Add the details to the hat, tassel, beard, and mustache.** Use a ⁵⁄₁₆" #6 gouge and a ³⁄₁₆" #11 veiner to shape the hat and tassel. Add a few spirals with the gouges where the hat folds over and hangs down. Use a ³⁄₈" #8 gouge to break up the flow of the beard a little more. Then deepen the grooves with a ³⁄₁₆" #11 veiner. Add more texture to the mustache with the same gouge. Make long, lazy S and C shapes when carving the beard and mustache. Avoid straight lines.

12 **Add the laugh lines around the eyes.** Sand the face lightly with 220-grit sandpaper to remove the tool marks. Remove the sanding dust and any sandpaper grit. Use a 70° ¹⁄₈" V-tool to create a few wrinkles at the corners of the eyes and in the bags underneath the eyes. If you get a ragged cut, try carving from the opposite direction. If you still get a ragged cut, hone your V-tool. Use a very small veiner in place of the V-tool for a softer look. These wrinkles make the eyes much more expressive.

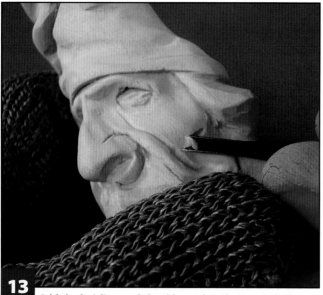

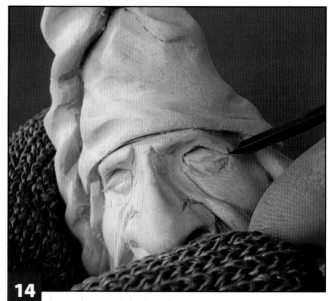

13 **Add the hairline and cheekbone details.** Use a 70° ¹⁄₈" V-tool. Carve along the hairline. Turn the cut in and curve under the cheekbones. The cut should meet the secondary smile line, even with the wing of the nostril. Then make another shallow cut to deepen the secondary smile line with the same V-tool. These cuts define the facial contours and make the carving look more realistic. This carving relies heavily on depth and shadows. A V-tool is the easiest way to add deep wrinkles and details.

14 **Carve the crow's feet at the outside corners of the eye.** Invert a ¼" #6 gouge, push it in at the top corner of the outside of the eye, and wiggle it back and forth to leave a mark. Turn the same gouge right side up and repeat the technique on the bottom corner. These cuts will be barely visible until you apply the final finish. The finish will pool in the cuts and accent them without making them unrealistically large. Use a detail knife to define the lower portion of the bags under the eyes.

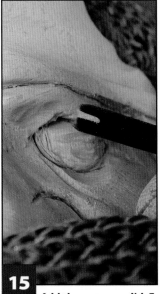
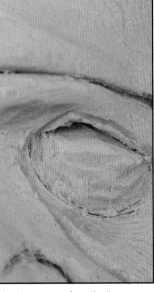

15 **Add the upper eyelid.** Test the sharpness of a 70° ⅛"
V-tool on a piece of scrap. If the V-tool is not perfectly sharp, the
tiny ridge of wood that makes up the eyelid will crumble away.
Remove a sliver of wood above the eye with the V-tool. Carve
close to, but not directly on, the line defining the eye. This cut
takes a bit of practice. I suggest you carve a few eyes on a piece
of scrap wood with a detail knife, and practice carving the upper
eyelid. One slip of the V-tool and the eyelid is gone for good.

16 **Add the final details to the beard and mustache.**
Deepen the grooves in the beard with a ³⁄₁₆" #11 veiner. Use the
same veiner to break up the edge at the bottom of the mustache.
Undercut below the mustache with a detail knife to lift the
mustache off the beard. Add more definition to the mustache
by cutting along the grooves with a 70° ⅛" V-tool. Remove a bit
more wood from the back of the beard with a ¹³⁄₁₆" #6 gouge. This
makes it easier to pierce through the beard in the next step.

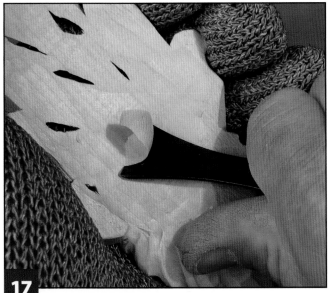

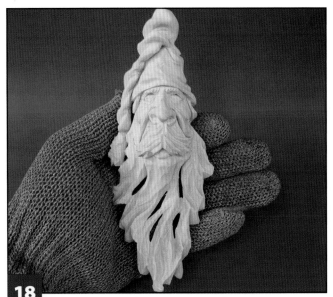

17 **Pierce through the beard.** Make several cuts in the deep
grooves of the beard with a 70° ¼" V-tool. If after several cuts you
still have not cut through the beard, hollow the back of the beard
a little more with a ¹³⁄₁₆" #6 gouge. Use caution, because the wood
is thin and fragile. Clean up the cuts, and blend them into the
other gouge grooves with a detail knife. These pierced cuts give
additional texture and dimension to the carving, and make it light
enough to be used as ornament.

18 **Refine the ornament.** View the carving from different
angles to spot any areas that need attention. Smooth the pierced
cuts and lightly sand the carving with 220-grit sandpaper to
take off any sharp edges. Be careful not to sand away the details.
Switch to 320-grit sandpaper to remove the scratches left by the
220-grit sandpaper. Burnish the carving with 400-grit sandpaper.
Brush off any dust or grit with a clean, dry brush. After you apply a
finish, the face will take on a soft look that resembles real skin.

Finishing the Santa

I use acrylic paint thinned with water to a stain-like consistency. Mix three drops of paint to 1½ ounces of warm water. Warm water helps the pigment dissolve.

Paint the lighter colors, such as the face, first. Dry the paint with a hair dryer after each color is applied. You can follow my color suggestions or make up your own color scheme.

After the paints dry, they will look dull, chalky, and barely visible. The next step is to dip the carving in boiled linseed oil (BLO). You can brush on the BLO, but this may cause the acrylic paint washes to bleed. Dipping the carving helps to prevent the bleeding. Pat off the excess oil with clean paper towels.

Immediately apply a couple coats of satin spray lacquer. Do not apply so much lacquer that it drips off the carving. Allow the lacquer to dry overnight. Smooth the lacquer by rubbing it with a crumpled-up brown paper bag. Remove any dust, and apply a mixture of equal parts dark and natural satin wax. Wipe off any excess wax with a paper towel, and allow the wax to dry for a few minutes. Then buff the carving to a high sheen with a soft buffing cloth.

Drill a hole in the top of the carving and insert your hook or hanger of choice.

Use caution when working with BLO. Oil soaked paper towels or rags can spontaneously combust. Soak the rags and towels in water inside a metal container until you can hang them outside to dry.

Olde World Santa pattern

Photocopy at 100%

CLEAN CUTS   tips

Don't try to hog off more wood than the gouge or veiner can handle. If the corners of the tool slip below the surface of the wood, the wood will tear, producing a rough cut. Use the largest tool possible to remove wood quickly without cutting too deep.

materials & tools

MATERIALS:
- 2¼" x 2¼" x 7" basswood
- ½" cup hook (for hanging)
- Sandpaper: 150, 220, 320, & 400 grits
- Acrylic paints:
  Alizarin crimson (hat)
  Antique white (beard, hair, mustache)
  White (hat tassel)
  Fleshtone (face and lips)
  Medium flesh (face and lips)
  Cadmium red (drybrush on high spots of face and lips)
- Satin finishing wax, dark and natural
- Boiled linseed oil
- Satin spray lacquer

TOOLS:
- Detail knife
- #6 gouges: ¼", 5⁄16", & 13⁄16"
- 3⁄8" #8 gouge
- #11 veiners: 1⁄8" & 3⁄16"
- 70° V-tools: 1⁄8" & ¼"

SPECIAL SOURCES:
Santa ornament blanks, roughouts, and a DVD with 90 minutes of step-by-step instructions for the ornament are available from *www.gargacsoriginals.com*, or 303-439-7201.

Candy Cane Squirrel Ornament

By Desiree Hajny

Given the right circumstances, realistic wildlife carvings make great holiday ornaments. I created this squirrel holding a candy cane to combine my interest in realistic wildlife with whimsical situations.

I carve this piece out of a solid block of wood using a variety of power and hand tools. After shaping the carving, add texture with power carving bits and a woodburner.

After you finish texturing the carving, mix a bit of water with burnt sienna acrylic paint and apply it to the squirrel with a round brush. Allow the paint to dry. Dip a stiff-bristle brush in white acrylic paint. Scrub the brush on a paper bag to remove most of

the paint and evenly distribute the remaining paint through the brush. Drybrush the squirrel with the white paint by stroking the brush across the fur texture. This adds contrast by highlighting only the raised texture in the fur.

Use a detail brush to paint the eyes and mouth black. Add a few dots of black to simulate whiskers and paint the teeth white. Use the detail brush to paint the red and white stripes on the candy cane.

This little squirrel gets caught trying to steal a candy cane from the Christmas tree.

Squirrel ornament patterns

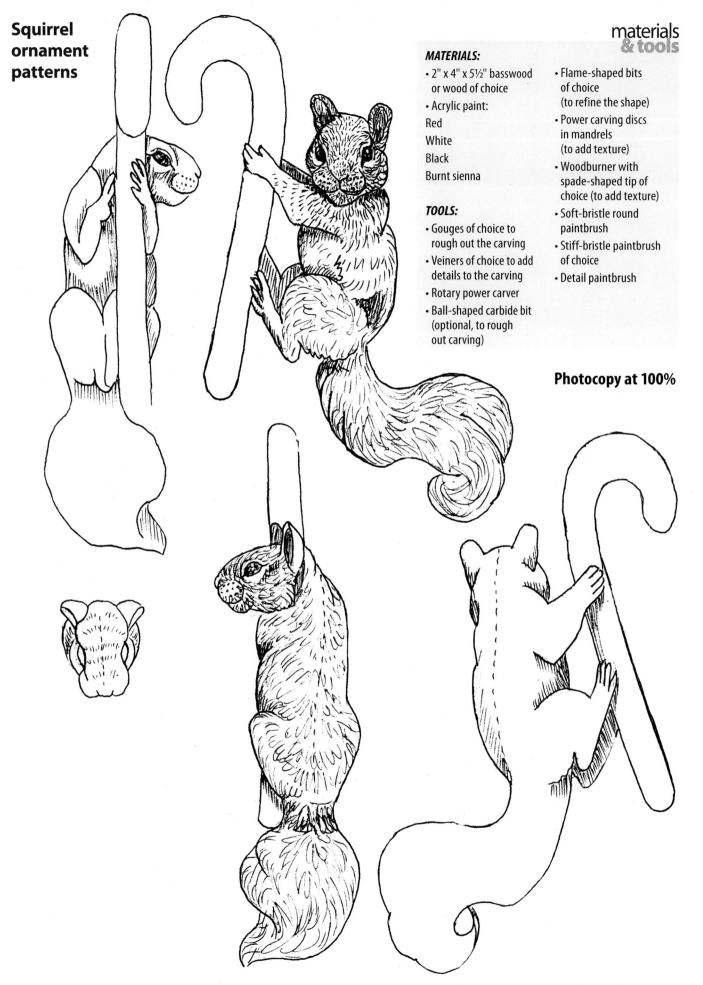

materials & tools

MATERIALS:
- 2" x 4" x 5½" basswood or wood of choice
- Acrylic paint:
  Red
  White
  Black
  Burnt sienna

TOOLS:
- Gouges of choice to rough out the carving
- Veiners of choice to add details to the carving
- Rotary power carver
- Ball-shaped carbide bit (optional, to rough out carving)
- Flame-shaped bits of choice (to refine the shape)
- Power carving discs in mandrels (to add texture)
- Woodburner with spade-shaped tip of choice (to add texture)
- Soft-bristle round paintbrush
- Stiff-bristle paintbrush of choice
- Detail paintbrush

Photocopy at 100%

Decorations

Whether you're decking your own halls or spreading holiday cheer to the homes of others, you're sure to find the perfect project in this chapter. Styles range from caricature to antique to folk art, with subjects from Santas to animals to trees, some super-simple for beginners and others challenging for experienced carvers. Even if you can't make all of the projects, you're sure to learn some great carving and finishing tips from the experts who created them.

Goodbye Kiss,
by Rick Jensen, page 76.

Simple Starter Santa

by Kathleen Schuck

This simple Santa can be carved in a day. It is a great project to become familiar with the position of facial features and is an ideal project for beginner carvers.

The project was inspired by a 74-year-old woman in one of my classes. She wanted to jump right into carving Santas. I was not sure she had the hand strength to complete the normal class Santa in the time allotted. Not wanting to disappoint her, I set out to design a simple Santa. My student was successful, and I have since carved several to test different color schemes for more elaborate Santas.

Most of my Santas are carved from 2" x 3" x 6" basswood blanks—it's a comfortable size to handle. Start by making a photocopy of the pattern. Trace the outside design onto the blank with graphite paper. Cut out the perimeter with a band saw, and replace the pattern over the blank to trace in the details.

Consider a pencil your #1 tool and mark the depth you want various parts of the Santa to be. Use an X to mark where to remove wood.

MAKING STOP CUTS **tips**

Do not undercut the facial features when making stop cuts. Aim the point of the knife toward the outside of the beard so you don't undercut it. When outlining the bridge of the nose, point the knife tip down toward the tip of the nose.

1

Remove the band saw marks. Use a carving knife to remove the sharp corners from the sides and back of the Santa. Round the sides. When you have an area to clean off that is wider than your knife, switch to a ½" #3 gouge. If you have a wider #3 gouge, use that. This will give you a better finished piece.

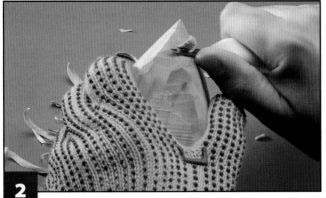

2 **Rough out the cloak.** Carve the back and front so the hood of the cloak comes to a peak in the middle of the 2" thickness. Then make a stop cut along the pattern lines of the cloak, arms, and hands with a ¼" V-tool. Use a knife to further define the stop cuts above and below the arms. Shave up to the stop cut at the bottom of the cloak and below the hands with a ½" #3 gouge so it looks like the cloak is over Santa's robe.

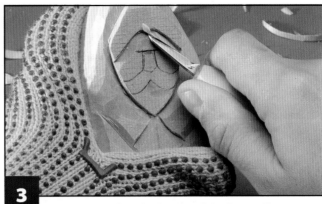

3 **Remove wood from both sides of the face.** Make a stop cut around the beard with a knife. Cut the wood away from the stop cuts on both sides of the face. Round the arms into the stop cuts above and below the arms. Remove wood from around the cowl to make it stand proud from the cloak. Make a stop cut around the cowl just above the forehead and remove enough wood so it appears that the head goes into and under the cowl.

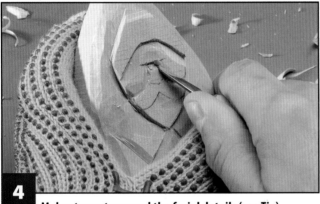

4 **Make stop cuts around the facial details (see Tip).** Make a deep stop cut at the line above the nose. Make a stop cut along the cheek line bordering the nose and top of the mustache. Taper the edges of the cheeks up to the stop cut. Angle the knife and cut the chip free at the top of the nose. Make a stop cut along the bottom of the mustache and taper the beard up to mustache.

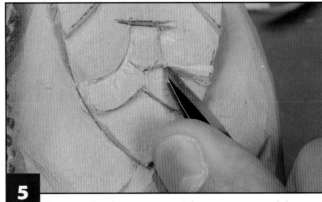

5 **Remove the sharp corners.** Make a stop cut around the tip of the nose. Round and shape the entire mustache to give it a smooth, flowing shape. Round and taper the forehead and cowl down into the cape. The cowl should be separated from, but flow toward, the cloak. Separate the hands by removing a wedge of wood from between them.

6 **Shape the eyes.** Hold your knife at an angle and slide the tip into the eye socket alongside the nose with the blade pointing to the outside of the face. Flick your wrist to bring the blade upward to cut a triangular chip from the nose to the stop cut above the nose. Use the same technique to carve the other eye.

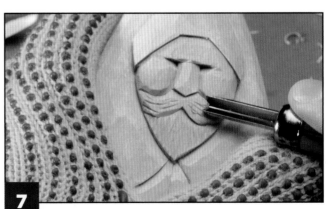

7 **Round the cheeks and the nose.** Round the nose down into the eye sockets with a knife. Round and shape the tip of the nose. Use the knife to round the cheeks down to the stop cuts on the outside of the face where the face meets the cloak. Use a V-tool to add hair lines for the beard and mustache.

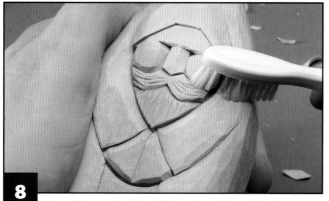

8 **Clean the carving.** Brush the carving with an old, clean toothbrush. If there are fingerprints, pencil marks, or dirt marks from oily hands, spray the carving with nontoxic all-purpose cleaner, and brush the soiled areas with the toothbrush. Rinse the carving in lukewarm water. Pat the carving off, and start painting before the carving dries. This keeps the grain from raising too much.

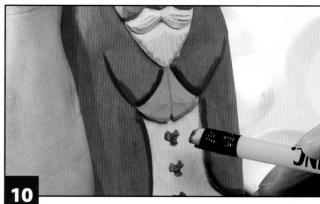

9 **Paint the Santa.** Add a few drops of flesh-colored paint to the palette well and fill the well with water. Stir it, and paint the hands and face. Use white for the beard and inner robe, a thinned light red for the cape, and a thinned dark red for the cowl. Put a dot of black paint in each chip-carved eye and add a tiny white dot at 11 o'clock or 7 o'clock. Add the white eyebrows.

Under and Over

Achieving depth and dimension is important in any carving. Think of what goes over (or outside) and under (or inside) on the carving. The mustache is under the nose and over the beard, so remove wood accordingly. Again, Santa's hands are over his cloak and go into his sleeves. Even subtle layers or depths add to the proportions of a carving.

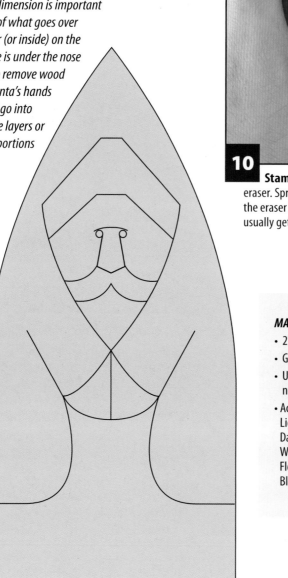

10 **Stamp the inner robe.** Cut a design into a soft, new pencil eraser. Spread a bit of paint on the flat center of the palette, dip the eraser into the paint and press the eraser onto the inner robe. I usually get two or three prints from each dip.

Starter Santa pattern

Photocopy at 100%

materials & tools

MATERIALS:
- 2" x 3" x 6" basswood
- Graphite paper
- Unsharpened pencil with a new eraser (eraser print)
- Acrylic paints:
  Light red
  Dark red
  White
  Flesh
  Black

TOOLS:
- Carving knife
- ½" #3 gouge
- ¼" V-tool
- Carving glove
- Paint brushes
- Paint palette

Carve and Paint an
Evergreen Tree

By Bob Mason

Carving trees is a lot of fun. It doesn't require a great deal of carving skill and the end results are really rewarding. Use the completed tree as a standalone project or create several trees to complement a holiday display.

I started carving trees four years ago. Prior to that, my carving experiences were mostly Santa Claus and other Christmas-themed items. I never thought I would be carving wood from a tree to make a tree. Of course, evergreen trees are an iconic symbol of Christmas, so maybe I haven't strayed too far.

1 **Transfer the pattern to the blank.** Draw a centerline on the front and right side of the blank and on the top of the block. Transfer the pattern to two adjacent sides of the blank with carbon paper. Use the centerlines as a guide. Make sure the horizontal lines connect on both sides of the blank. Mark the depth lines in red.

My first trees were small, ranging from 4" to 6" tall. It wasn't long until I was getting orders for trees up to 12" tall. The technique is the same no matter what size tree you are carving, and the pattern is easy to adapt to a variety of sizes. This demonstration uses a 3" by 3" by 8" block. Use the pattern provided or create your own pattern for an alternative size tree. Experiment with creating tall skinny trees and short fat trees. The only rule is that the width and thickness of the block must be equal.

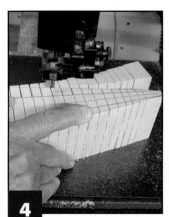

2 **Create a wedge.** Create a wedge to keep the blank square as you cut the waste wood from the tree. Use the pattern to transfer one of the perimeter lines to a piece of scrap wood and cut the wedge shape with a band saw.

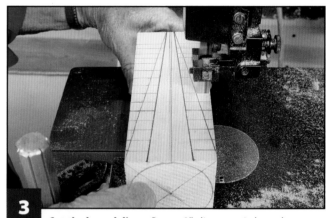

3 **Cut the branch lines.** Draw a 3"-diameter circle on the bottom of the blank. Cut in along each branch line with a band saw. Do not cut past the depth line. Make four series of cuts, cutting along the branch lines on the front and side of the blank.

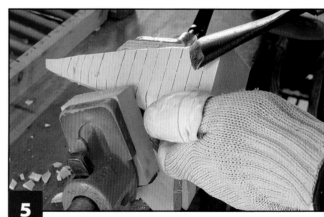

4 **Cut the perimeter lines.** Cut along the two black perimeter lines on the front of the blank. Then rotate the blank 90°. Use the wedge to keep the blank square to the table. Offset the wedge to keep it out of the blade's cutting path. Cut the first perimeter line, reposition the wedge, and cut the second line.

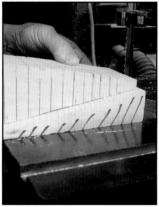

5 **Round the pyramid.** Secure the blank in a vise or with a bench hook. Use a 70mm #7 gouge, a 35mm #3 gouge, or a draw knife to turn the pyramid into a cone. Use the largest tool you have. Use the circle on the bottom as a guide.

6 **Carve the layers of branches.** Work from the top of the tree down. Use a 16mm #3 palm gouge or a reciprocating carver with a 15mm #3 gouge to taper each layer toward the center of the tree. Start the upward cut about ⅛" above the saw cut. This gives the impression of bent branches.

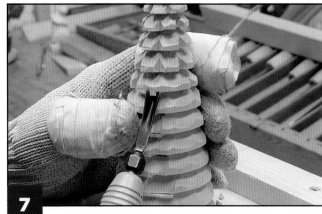

7 **Separate the limbs.** Use a 10mm 75° V-tool to separate the branches into limbs. The limbs start small near the top and get larger as you move down the tree. Go back over the cuts with a 6mm 75° V-tool and cut as far up the branch into the tree as possible to add depth and shadows.

8 **Shape and texture the limbs.** Make a deep cut through the center of each limb with a 3mm #10 gouge. Carve three slanted lines on each side of the U-cut with a 6mm 75° V-tool.

9 **Shape the top of the tree.** Carve the tip of the tree with a knife. Go back and make a series of random cuts with a 6mm 75° V-tool to create shadows.

10 **Clean up the carving.** Lightly cut between each layer of branches with a hacksaw to emphasize the separate layers. Smooth each branch with a sander wheel in a drill.

11 **Mount the tree on a base.** Mount the finished tree on a ½"-thick circle of wood. The diameter of the circle is ¾" less than the diameter of the base of the tree. Sign and date your work on the side of the base. For small trees, use ¼"-thick circles.

12 **Apply a base coat.** Thin evergreen paint heavily with water and flood the carving with the paint wash. I hold it over a plastic container. It may take several coats of paint to get a rich dark green.

13 **Let the base coat dry.** Hold the carving in a towel and blast it with 130 pounds of air pressure to keep the grain from raising. Let the paint dry for several days.

14 **Add the snow.** Use white straight from the bottle. Apply the paint with a ¼"-wide flat brush. Start at the top of the tree and apply the paint heavily using the side of the brush. Use a lighter application for the upper and middle branches. Apply the paint heavier on the bottom branches.

materials & tools

MATERIALS:
- 8½" x 11" graph paper ¼"-scale (optional, to create your own patterns)
- Carbon paper
- 3" x 3" x 8" basswood
- Scrap wood (wedge)
- ½" x 3" x 3" basswood (circle base)
- Acrylic paints:
  Evergreen
  Pure white

TOOLS:
- Band saw
- 35mm #3 gouge (or larger)
- Reciprocating power carver (optional)

- 15 mm #3 gouge
- 10mm 75° V-tool
- 6mm 75° V-tool
- 3mm #10 U-gouge
- Carving knife
- Hacksaw blade
- Drill and sander wheel
- ½"-wide flat brush
- 1"- to 2"-wide foam paintbrush
- Air compressor

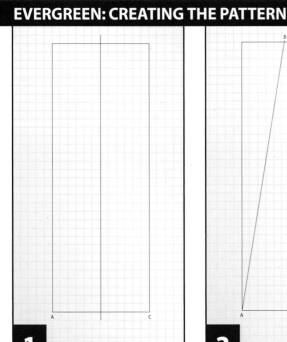

1 **Determine the size of the project.** I use ¼" graph paper. Start by drawing a rectangle indicating the overall height and width desired. Sketch in a vertical centerline. Label the bottom corners A and C.

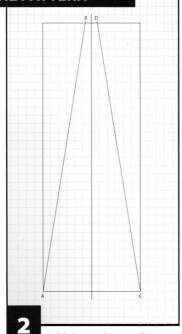

2 **Add the perimeter lines.** The top of the tree will be ⅜" wide. Make a mark ³⁄₁₆" on either side of the centerline. Label these marks B and D. Draw a line from point A to point B. Draw a second line from point C to point D.

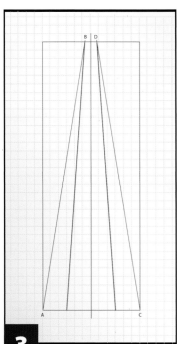

3 **Add the depth lines.** Make a mark ¾" in toward the centerline from points A and C. Draw a red line from each of these two points up to points B and D. These red depth lines will be used to guide the band saw cuts.

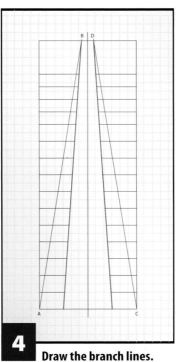

4 **Draw the branch lines.** The top does not have branches. The branches at the bottom are wider. Draw lines about ½" apart. The branches on the top are narrower. Draw these lines about ⅜" apart. Extend the lines on either side of the depth lines.

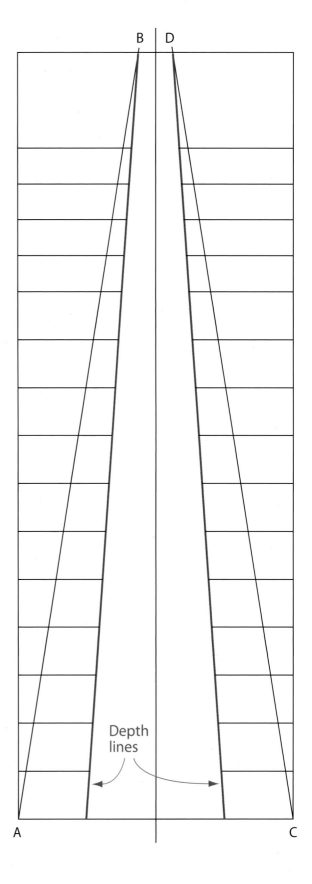

Depth lines

Hand Carving a
Simple Reindeer

By Don Swartz
*Step-by-step photos
by Bob Duncan*

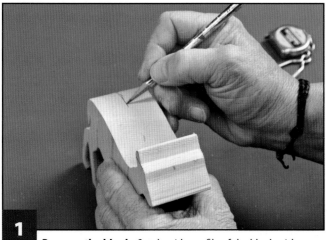

1 **Prepare the blank.** Cut the side profile of the blank with a band saw. Draw a centerline the whole way around the blank. Use the band saw to separate the legs.

Carve this rustic deer as a standalone project or size the pattern to create the perfect complement to your favorite carved Santa. Use twigs for the antlers to add to the rustic charm and simplify the carving process.

I use knives, chisels, and gouges to carve the deer, leaving the tool marks visible. Use power carving tools or sand away the tool marks and woodburn fur texture for a more realistic reindeer.

Create a herd of deer and give one a red nose in honor of Santa's favorite reindeer, Rudolph. Add leather reigns and position the deer in front of a sleigh for a dramatic mantel display.

The pattern for this reindeer is based on drawings in *Doug Lindstrand's Alaska Sketchbook.*

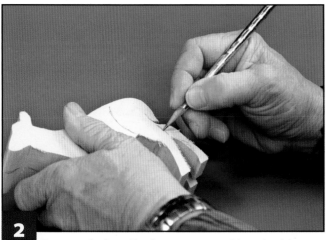

2 **Draw on the legs.** Use the pattern as a guide to sketch in the legs. Shade the waste portion of the legs with a pencil.

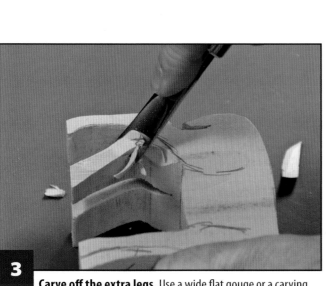

3 **Carve off the extra legs.** Use a wide flat gouge or a carving knife. Remove the waste wood to produce four individual legs.

4 **Rough out the tail.** Sketch in the tail and use a carving knife to make a stop cut on both sides of the tail. Carve in to the stop cut from both sides to outline the tail.

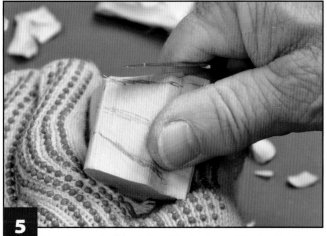

5 **Rough out the head.** Sketch in the taper of the head and remove the extra wood with a carving knife.

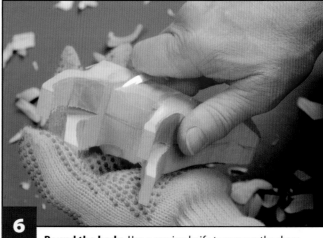

6 **Round the body.** Use a carving knife to remove the sharp corners, rounding the neck, back, sides, and belly.

7 **Separate the head from the neck.** Draw the jaw line. Make a stop cut along the line with a carving knife and taper the neck up to the stop cut.

8 **Shape the legs.** Draw in the areas where the legs intersect with the body and remove wood from both sides of the legs. Taper the legs down to the hooves.

9 **Carve the area between the legs.** Use a ½" #5 palm gouge. This area is mostly end grain and can be difficult to carve.

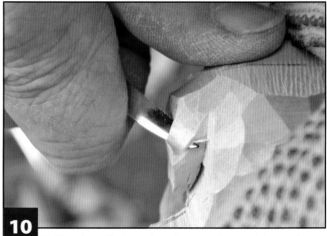

10 **Refine the tail.** Carve the tail into an elongated diamond shape. Use a carving knife.

11 Refine the legs. Taper the legs down close to where the hooves flare out. Use a ½" #7 gouge and a carving knife. Use centerlines to create a rough diamond shape.

12 Carve the front shoulder. Mark the areas where the legs, body, and neck meet. Carve a groove along the line to simulate the shoulders with a ½" #7 gouge.

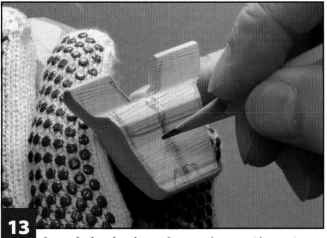

13 Carve the head and ears. Separate the ears with a carving knife. Taper the face and mark the location of the nose and eyes.

14 Refine the ears. Shape the ears using the pattern as a guide. Use a ¼" #5 gouge to hollow out the inside of the ears.

15 Carve the nose and mouth. Use a small veiner to carve along the mouth line. Remove a bit of wood from the bottom jaw. Press the veiner into the nose area to make stop cuts around the nostrils. Carve up to the stop cuts to hollow out the nostrils.

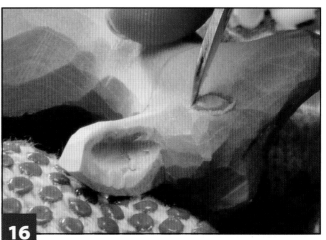

16 Carve the eyes. Use the tip of a knife to make a shallow stop cut around the perimeter of each eye. Then relieve up to the stop cuts to separate the eyeballs from the eyelids. Carefully round each eyeball.

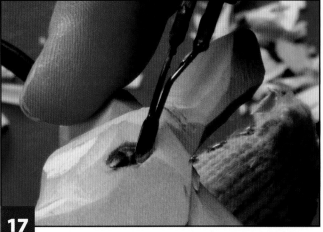

17 **Woodburn the facial details.** Use a woodburner to clean up the cuts around the eyes and nose, and lightly burn in the nose. Burn the mouth line and darken the nostrils and eyeballs.

18 **Finish carving the hooves.** Separate the hooves from the legs with a carving knife. Shape the hooves so they are slightly smaller than the fetlocks and lower legs. Use a small V-tool to add a shallow groove to the front of each hoof.

20 **Drill the holes for the antlers.** Use a ⅛"-diameter drill bit to carefully drill holes for the antlers. Cut fresh twigs to represent the antlers and bend them to shape. Glue the antlers in place after you are finished painting.

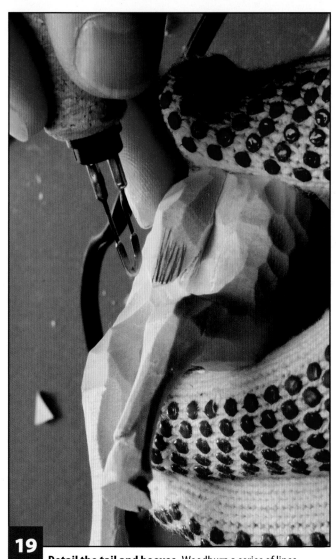

19 **Detail the tail and hooves.** Woodburn a series of lines to simulate hair on the tail. Lightly shade the hooves with a woodburner and burn in the groove on the front of each hoof.

Painting the Reindeer

Mist the entire carving with water before painting. I use acrylic paints thinned with water. Use skin tone base for the belly and burnt umber for the back. Use smoked pearl on the sides to transition between the light and dark brown. Use a hair dryer to speed up the drying process. Apply a very thin wash of raw sienna to the entire carving to further blend the colors. Do not paint the eyes, nose, mouth, or hooves. Seal the carving with clear or clear satin spray finish; a spray lacquer; or your finish of choice.

materials
& tools

MATERIALS:

- 1½" x 5" x 5¼" basswood, clear white pine, or jelutong
- 2 each fresh twigs
- Acrylic paints:
  Smoked pearl
  Skin tone base
  Burnt umber
  Raw sienna
- Clear or clear satin spray finish, spray lacquer, or finish of choice

TOOLS:

- Carving knife
- Wide flat gouge
- #5 palm gouges: ¼", ½"
- ½" #7 gouge
- Small veiner
- Small V-tool
- Woodburner with a skew tip
- Assorted paintbrushes
- Drill with ⅛"-diameter bit

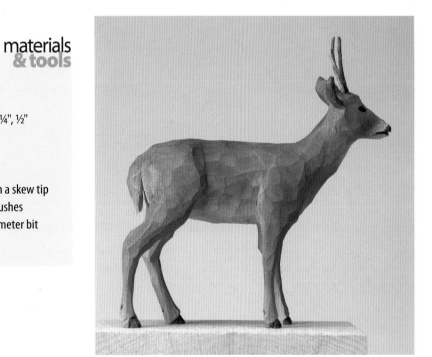

Simple reindeer patterns

Photocopy at 100%

Santa
with
Cardinal

By Vicki Bishop

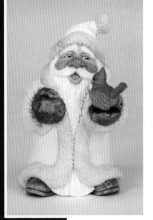

In this charming caricature, Santa takes time out from his hectic schedule to visit with a feathered friend. You can carve several of the cardinals separately and use them as miniature ornaments for your Christmas tree or wreath.

I decided to do this Santa in white and blue and add a splash of red with the bird. I really don't like to paint white because it always looks ceramic. The white can't be used as a wash because it looks dirty, so I have to mix it 50/50 with water. I use wood bleach to strip the color from the wood and then paint the sections with the color. Safety is important. I wear a cut-resistant glove and a thumb guard.

Step 1: Transfer the pattern to the blank. Then cut out one profile on the band saw. Tape the pieces you cut off back onto the blank, using double-sided tape. Then cut out the other profile.

Step 2: Rough shape the piece. I use a 1⅞" bench knife and a ⅝" #9 gouge. I work all over the piece trying to shape it—not detail it. I can't stress this enough.

Step 3: Draw on the details with a pencil. Go back, and carve off the pencil lines with a ¼" 60° V-tool. This keeps the carving cleaner; sets the carving into a 3D view so you can make changes before stop cuts; and gives your knife a V-groove to follow.

Step 4: Make stop cuts at each V-tool line. Use a bench knife. Carve away areas that need to be relieved.

Step 5: Add the wrinkles to the bends of the arms. Start with a 6mm #11 veiner. Deepen some wrinkles with a ¼" 60° V-tool. The V-tool adds deeper shadow to some of the wrinkles; in this case less is more.

Step 6: Detail the fur. Round it off with a bench knife. Then cut in a diagonal across the grain with a ⅛" 60° V-tool to detail the fur. Make short strokes from the middle in both directions so you don't tear the wood.

Step 7: Shape the hair and beard. After the initial shaping with a bench knife, use a 6mm #11 veiner to establish the depth and flow of the hair and beard. Go back in with a 2mm #11 veiner. Finish the hair and fur with little triangular cuts along the edges to give shadow and the illusion of separation.

Step 8: Add facets to the coat. Go back over the coat with a ⅝" #9 gouge. These facets will give depth to the surface.

Step 9: Bleach the whole carving with a two-part wood bleach. Follow the manufacturer's instructions, but leave the bleach on for eight hours. Bleach the carving a total of three times before neutralizing the bleach with white vinegar. Allow the carving to dry overnight.

Painting Santa

The formulas for mixing paint are based on a round bubble tray that holds 1 teaspoon of water. I use a Loew-Cornell #3 synthetic round brush for most of the carving

and an #18/0 liner is used for the eyes. Be careful not to overload the brush to keep the paint from bleeding into the bleached areas.

Step 10: Paint the skin. Mix 1 drop of Caucasian flesh and 2 drops of medium flesh with 1 teaspoon of water.

Step 11: Add the blush to the cheeks. Mix 1 drop of tomato spice with ½ teaspoon of water.

Step 12: Paint the fur. Mix 3 drops blue heaven with 1 teaspoon water.

Step 13: Paint the mittens and boots. Add 1 drop of black to 1 teaspoon of water.

Step 14: Paint the eyes. Paint a line of undiluted black at the top of the eyeball, avoiding the eyelid. Dry with a hair dryer between each step. Then paint the eyeball with undiluted white leaving the thin line of black at the top of the eye. Paint a solid semicircle of undiluted black on top of the white. Then paint undiluted blue heaven on top of the black, leaving a thin line of black showing. Paint a small circle of undiluted black on top of the blue for a pupil. Finally, dot white on the eyeball where the blue of the iris and black pupil meet on parallel sides of the eye.

Step 15: Paint the cardinal. Add four drops of tompte red with one teaspoon of water for the body. Thin yellow with enough water to make it flow easily for the beak. Then shade around the eyes with black.

Step 16: Antique the carving. Allow the paint to dry totally. Then mix ¼" squeezed out of a tube of artists' oil burnt sienna with a small amount of boiled linseed oil. Add this mixture to the rest of the quart of boiled linseed oil. Paint the antiquing oil on the face, mittens, boots, and

bird. Do not get any of the oil on the bleached areas. Allow the oil to dry for three days.

Step 17: Seal the carving. Spray the carving with satin clear wood finish.

material & tools

MATERIALS:
- 4" x 4" x 6" basswood
- 2-part wood bleach
- Acrylic paints:
  Caucasian flesh
  Medium flesh
  Tomato spice
  Blue heaven
  Black
  White
  Tompte red
  Yellow
- Boiled linseed oil
- Artists' oil paint: Burnt sienna
- #3 synthetic round brush
- #18/0 liner brush
- Bubble pallet
- Satin clear spray finish

TOOLS:
- 1⅞" bench knife
- 6mm #11 veiner
- 2mm #11 veiner
- ⅝" #9 gouge
- ¼" 60° V-tool
- ⅛" 60° V-tool

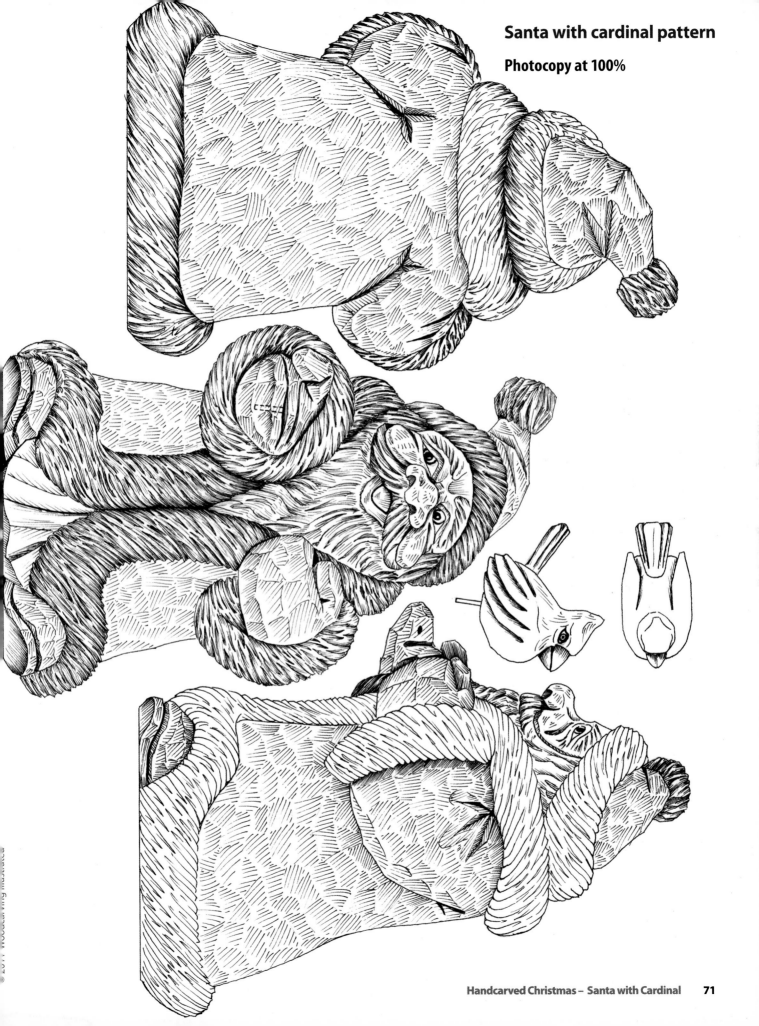

Herby's Angel

by Paul McLeod

Herby Ham designed his angel with beginner carvers in mind.

materials & tools

MATERIALS:
- 2½" x 3½" x 5½" basswood block (angel)
- ¼" x ¾" x 1¼" basswood scrap (book)
- Finish of choice (I use boiled linseed oil)

TOOLS:
- Carving knife of choice (I use a 2¼" blade)
- ¹⁄₁₆" and ⁵⁄₃₂" V-tools (outlining hair, shawl, and sash)
- ¾" 45° V-tool (groove between wings in back)
- ⅛" #11 and ¼" #11 gouges (pleats in skirt and shawl)
- ¼" #9 fishtail gouge (top inside of wings)
- ½" #5 and #7 gouges (inside of wings)

SPECIAL SOURCES:
Roughouts for Herby's Angel are available from *www.whiterivercrafts.com*, or 870-941-8740.

Herby Ham designed this charming angel. Herby is responsible for starting my love affair with carving wood, and I know that he would be honored to have the piece featured to inspire other carvers.

I met Herby in the late 1990s while wintering in Uvalde, Texas. Herby had renovated a large building with donated materials and labor and turned it into a senior center with more than 3,000 square feet dedicated to the wood shop.

My wife and I decided to stay for awhile, and I spent most of my time helping other "winter Texans" with their woodworking projects and repairing various woodworking machines. Herby finally convinced me to try woodcarving. Of course I said what most people say—I can't do that. He encouraged me to give it a shot and with his guidance, I discovered a new hobby, and have been carving ever since.

Sometime later, I found out that my stepmother's aunt was Herby's grandmother. I suppose that made us "kissin' cousins." Herby died several years ago, and my wife and I stayed in Uvalde helping out at the center. Herby's wife, Nancy, gave me permission to use Herby's Angel for my woodcarving teaching and sales and for publication. The angel is a tribute to a fine man who helped many folks discover the joy of woodcarving.

Carving Herby's Angel

Herby's Angel is carved out of a solid block of wood. Herby would cut out the side-view pattern on the bandsaw, but would carve the other profiles. Herby's method took two days of hard carving to finish the angel. Since I teach with Herby's Angel, I had roughouts made, so it only takes one day of moderately hard carving to finish it.

No special tools are needed to carve the angel; however, a scoop-type (fishtail) short-bent gouge helps with the inside of the wings. Other than the wings, the angel is not difficult to carve.

Carve the outside of the wings first. Do not make the insides of the wings concave near the edge; it makes them more difficult to carve. A uniform curve from the inside edge to the back of the shawl is the best way to carve the wings.

The book that may be placed in the Angel's hands was the idea of Norman "Norm" Rutledge, one of the participants in my angel carving class at the North Arkansas Woodcarvers Club in Mountain Home, Arizona.

Angel patterns

Photocopy at 100%

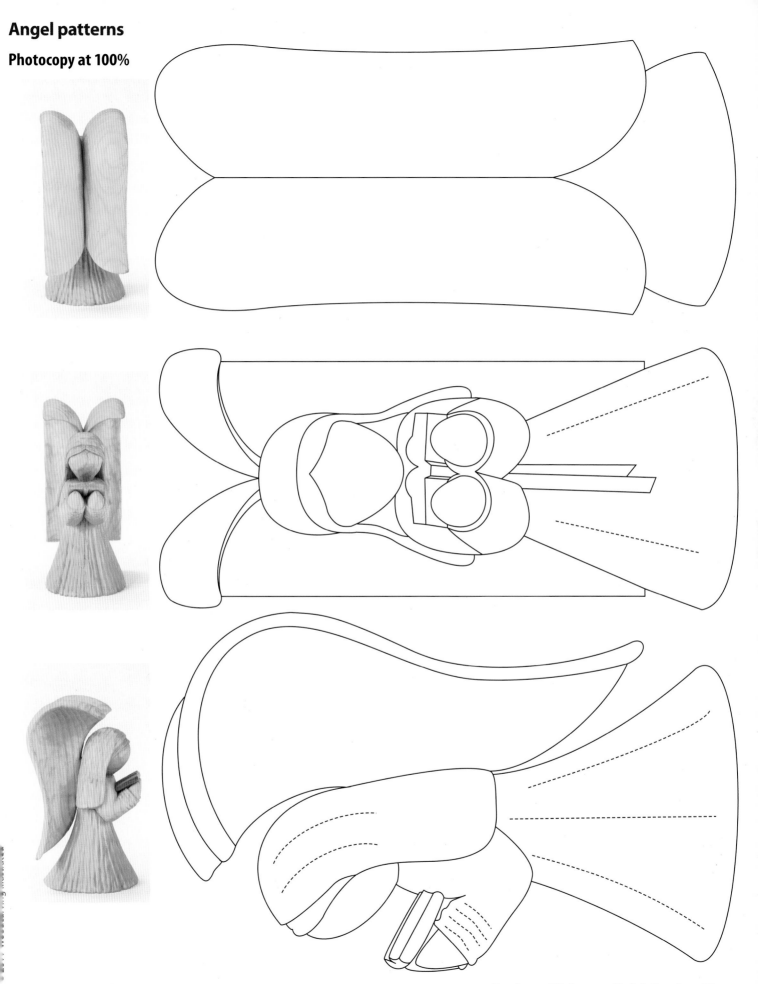

Folk Art Santa

by Rick Jensen

I prefer cottonwood bark for most of my carvings because of its lack of difficult grain and rich, red color. The sanding method gives the carving a worn look and allows the reddish-brown tones of the bark to show through. Use centerlines to maintain proper proportions. I align the front centerline parallel with the grain to strengthen the nose.

Antique Finish Gives Santa the Look of a Treasured Heirloom

I use acrylic paints thinned with water to the consistency of a stain. Re-coat areas where a stronger color is desired. Use a #10 round brush for most of the painting and a #6 flat or shader brush for dry brushing.

Paint the face with thinned medium flesh. While the paint is wet, add a full-strength dab of red iron oxide to the cheeks, tip of the nose, and the mouth. Lightly blend it in with a flat brush. The hair, beard, and mustache are painted with thinned ivory. Paint the eyebrows with a slightly thicker ivory paint. Use a thinned burnt sienna for the mittens and the inner robe. Paint the wreath deep river green. Dry brush it, using ivory and a flat brush. Use thinned mendocino red to color the robe and hat including the trim areas. Combine one drop of metallic gold paint with two drops of flow medium. Use this mixture to paint over the trim on the robe, the hatband, and the belt.

Allow the carving to dry completely. Lightly sand off some of the paint on the high spots of the carving, excluding the face, with 120-grit sandpaper. This allows the color of the bark to show in those areas and gives Santa a shabby-chic look.

Spray the carving with spray lacquer. Allow the first coat to dry; then rub the carving with a crumpled-up brown paper bag. Remove any dust from the carving. Keep applying coats until you build up an even sheen. If it becomes too shiny, use matte spray finish to eliminate the glossy sheen.

Use a 50/50 mix of dark and natural satin finishing wax to antique the carving. Make sure the wax is well mixed, and apply it liberally to the whole carving with a 1" china bristle brush. Wipe off the carving and the brush with a cotton rag. Use the brush to clean out any areas where the wax pooled. Allow the wax to dry for a minimum of 24 hours; then buff the carving using a shoe brush or a rotary horsehair brush.

Carving Cottonwood Bark

Cottonwood bark doesn't carve like ordinary wood. As with any unfamiliar medium, it's important to practice. Keep the following tips in mind as you explore this versatile medium.

- **Glue together several pieces of bark.** *You can easily create a blank of appropriate dimensions or adjust the pattern size to fit the stock you have.*

- **Don't rely on stop cuts.** *The lack of grain and crumbly texture prevent stop cuts from being the barrier they are in ordinary wood. If you push too hard, the tool will slip right past.*

- **Use cyanoacrylate (CA) glue to strengthen soft areas.** *Cottonwood bark can have some downright crumbly areas. If you hit an area like this, soak it with CA glue, let it dry, and carve away.*

- **Sharp tools are required.** *Cottonwood bark is unforgiving. A dull tool will compress fibers and produce rough cuts. Spend some extra time honing and polishing your tools.*

- **Cottonwood bark tends to fuzz.** *No matter how careful you are and how sharp your tools are, cottonwood bark is going to have a few fuzzy areas. I use radial bristle discs to remove these fuzzies. Chuck several of the discs on a power-carving mandrel. Use the discs at a low speed to remove the fuzzies and soften the sharp edges.*

materials & tools

MATERIALS:
- 2¾" x 2¼" x 10" cottonwood bark
- Acrylic paints:
  Red iron oxide
  Metallic gold
  Medium flesh tone
  Mendocino red
  Burnt sienna
  Deep river green
  Ivory
- Flow medium
- Sandpaper, 120 grit
- Semi-gloss clear wood finish
- Matte spray finish
- Satin finishing wax, dark and neutral
- Cotton rag
- Brown paper bag

TOOLS:
- 1⅞" bench knife
- 1" #5 gouge
- 4mm #11 gouge
- 2mm #11 gouge
- ½" #3 gouge
- 12mm 75° V-tool
- Radial bristle disk, red, 220 grit
- #10 round brush
- #6 shader (flat) brush
- 1" china bristle brush
- Shoe brush or rotary horsehair brush

Goodbye Kiss

By Rick Jensen

The inspiration for these pieces was a picture of Santa my mother had; my original carvings were a present to her many years ago. I carve Santa Claus and Mrs. Claus (aka Kitty—bet you didn't know her name!) from basswood and color them with acrylic paint. I seal them with a laquer finish and add an antiquing wax to give them a soft, satiny, want-to-be-touched, finish. Practice carving Kitty's "kissing lips" on scrap wood; they are the most difficult part of the carving.

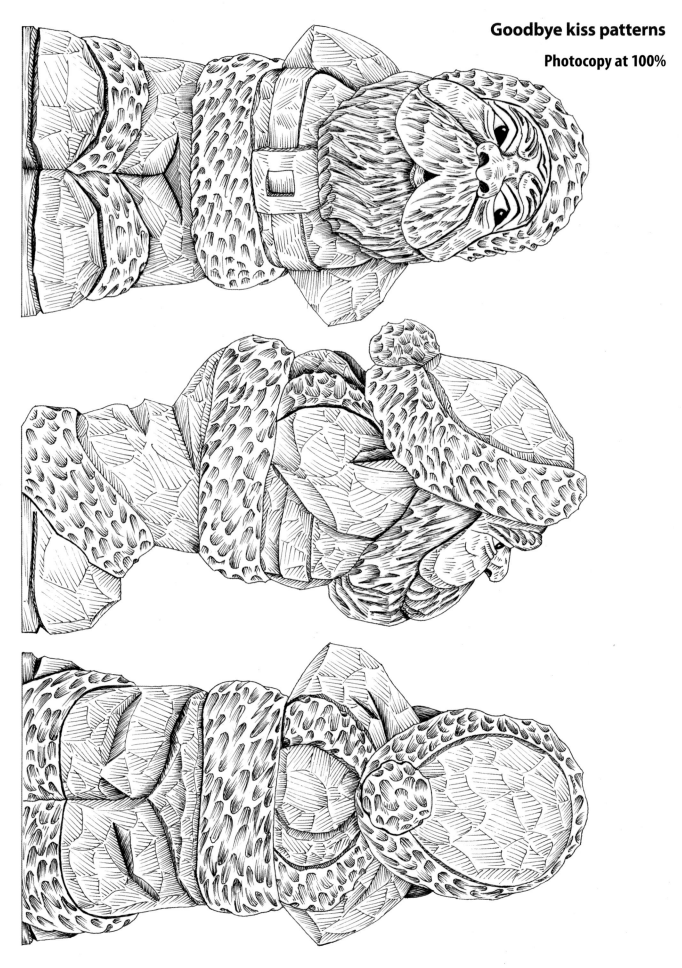

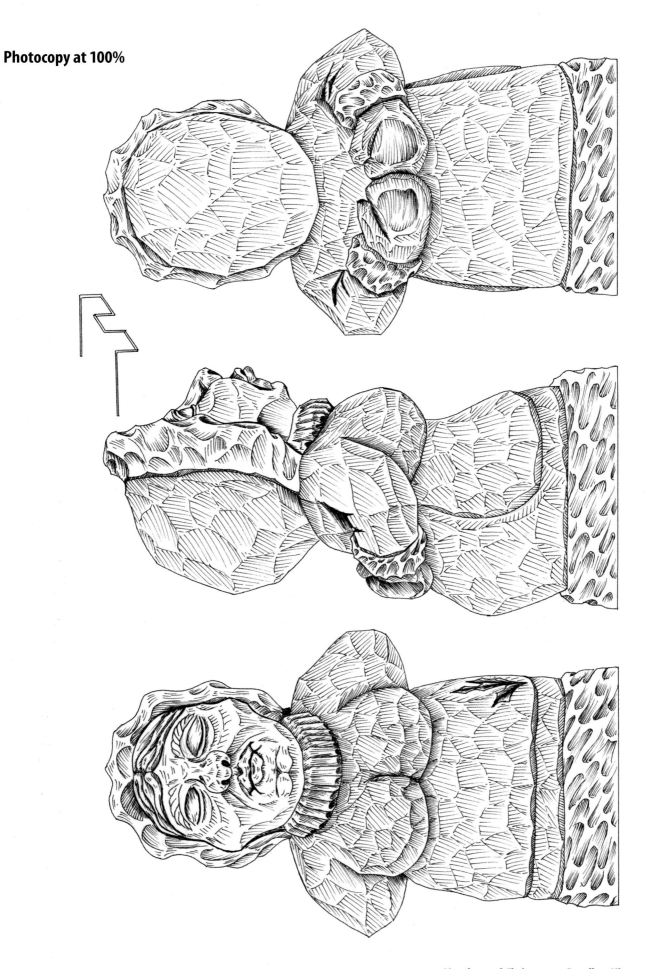

Santa Collector's Plate

By Robert Biermann

This carving is done in intaglio style, which is a type of relief carving. Traditional relief carving removes the wood around the subject so the subject protrudes from the wood. Intaglio carving lowers the subject, not the background.

Start with a 12"-diameter flat beaded basswood plate. Photocopy the pattern and cut off the excess paper. Align the pattern so the grain runs across the design from side to side. Transfer the pattern to the plate with graphite paper and a stylus.

Carving the Design

Position a 45° V-tool on the perimeter of the face. Tilt the V-tool so the outer wing—the side facing away from the face—is perpendicular to the wood. Outline the entire face with the V-tool. Hold the V-tool normally and outline the leaves and berries.

Carve the rest of the face using ordinary relief-carving techniques. Use #11 veiners and #3 gouges for most of the carving. The #11 veiner produces softer cuts than a V-tool.

The most difficult part is creating the sides of the nose and the eye mounds. Carve up the side of the nose into the eye area with a 5mm #11 veiner to rough out each eye mound. Use #11 veiners to carve the hair and beard for a soft flowing look.

The final stage of carving is to make sure there are no fuzzies or chatter marks left by dull tools. Keep your tools sharp to avoid a lot of cleanup work.

Finishing the Plate

The first step to finishing is to apply a boiled linseed oil (BLO) finish. Coat the entire plate with oil and wipe it off with paper towels. Be sure to remove any wet spots. Spread the oily towels outdoors to dry before discarding them in the household trash. Allow the BLO to dry for a day before sealing the plate with clear matte finish. After the sealer dries, you can start painting.

Leave most of the face the natural color of the BLO-finished wood. Shade the sides of the face and under the hat with burnt sienna. Blend the burnt sienna out from the shadows so there are no hard lines. Add a bit of cadmium red to the cheeks to give them a rosy glow.

Add a light wash of primary yellow to the beard and allow it to dry. Pick up a bit of white paint with a flat shader brush. Dry-brush the white over the beard by holding the brush at a 45° angle and dragging it lightly across the beard. This keeps the white paint on the top of the beard, giving a shadow effect to the textured areas.

Finish painting the carving using the photo as a guide. I use blue heaven for the irises and black for Santa's pupils. Apply a base coat to the hat, leaves, and berries and then shade them with the darker color after the base coat is dry. Seal the carving with two more coats of clear matte finish.

Display the plate in a stand or add hardware to the back to hang the plate on a wall.

The subject is recessed with the high points, such as Santa's nose, closest to the surface and the uncarved background.

Santa plate pattern

Pattern is drawn
to scale on a 1" grid.
Enlarge or reduce
to desired size.

MATERIALS:

- 12"-diameter beaded
  basswood plate (available at
  woodcarving supply stores)
- Graphite paper
- Boiled linseed oil
- Clear matte finish
- Acrylic paints:
  Burnt sienna (face shading
  Antique white (beard, eyes)
  White (beard)

Black (eyes)
Blue heaven (eyes)
Iron oxide (hat)
Gamal green (leaves)
Black green (leaf shading)
Primary yellow (beard)
Cadmium red (rosy cheeks)
Black plum (hat and
berries shading)

materials & tools

TOOLS:

- Stylus
- 6mm 45° V-tool
- #3 gouges: 3mm,
  5mm, & 8mm
- #11 gouges: 4mm,
  5mm, & 7mm
- Carving knife of choice
  (to clean up cuts)

Special Delivery Santa

By Doug Stewart

About 15 years ago, I carved my first large Santa for my wife on our anniversary. Since then, I have been customizing my gifts by carving individual toys for Santa's bag, choosing them based on the recipient's hobbies, career, or interests.

Preparing the Stock

This Santa is 18" tall, but the pattern can be scaled to fit any size wood. To get a block this size, I glue and clamp together four 2" x 10" x 18" pieces of basswood. Flatten and smooth two adjoining sides with a hand plane, sander, or jointer to make it easier to transfer the pattern views onto the blank. Trace the pattern on the front and side and cut the front profile with a band saw. Save the large pieces of waste and reattach them to the blank with masking tape. This makes it easier to cut the side profile.

Carving Santa

Rough-shape the carving with a 20mm #3 gouge. Pay close attention to the location of the arm and bag. Work around the whole carving to keep everything in proportion. When you're satisfied with the overall shape, start detailing the coat. Outline the cuffs and add wrinkles and folds to the coat. Continue to add details to the coat and bag, finishing with the belt.

Move on to the face. Separate the beard from the face and shape the beard. Add rough flow to the beard with a 3mm V-tool. Use a 1.5mm V-tool to add texture to the beard. Shape the nose using your tools of choice. Sketch in the eyes with a pencil and carve along the lines with a 1.5mm V-tool.

Carve the walking stick separately and drill a hole through Santa's hand. Carefully sand the carving with 220-grit sandpaper to remove any fuzz and soften the facets. Do not sand off or flatten the details and tool marks. After sanding, wash the carving with warm water and a soft scrub brush. Allow it to air dry.

Finishing Santa

Mix equal parts of satin lacquer and lacquer thinner. Apply two coats of the mixture to the carving to harden the surface so the paint goes on smoother. Remove any remaining fuzz in the creases of the carving with a carving knife or sandpaper.

I use acrylic paint. Use barn red for the coat, ivory for the white areas, and black for the gloves and belt. Use deep river green for the under robe and gold metallic for the trim and belt buckle. Use flesh for the face; mix a bit of red with the flesh for the rosy cheeks and nose. The eyes are painted with sky blue with a dot of navy blue for the pupil. I apply golden oak or pecan stain to the walking stick.

After the paint and stain dry, lightly sand the carving with 220-grit sandpaper. This exposes the wood on the sharper edges of the carving and gives it a worn appearance. Stain the entire carving with golden oak or pecan stain to bring out the details. Apply three coats of spray satin lacquer. Rub the carving with 0000 steel wool between the coats of lacquer.

The toys are created in the same fashion. Cut the individual toys out on a band saw first and then carve them to shape. Paint each toy and antique them using the techniques above.

Patterns are drawn to scale on a 1" grid. Enlarge or reduce to desired size.

Customize Santa with individual toys carved specifically for the recipient.

materials & tools

MATERIALS:

- 4 each 2" x 10" x 18" basswood or wood of choice or 8" x 10" x 18" basswood or wood of choice
- Assorted small pieces of wood (toys)
- Acrylic paints:
  Barn red
  Ivory
  Black
  Deep river green
  Flesh
  Sky blue
  Navy blue
- Golden oak or pecan stain
- Satin brush-on lacquer
- Lacquer thinner
- Spray satin lacquer
- 0000 steel wool
- Sandpaper, 220 grit

TOOLS:

- 20mm #3 gouge
- 12mm #8 gouge
- 10mm 60° V-tool
- 3mm 60° V-tool
- 1.5mm 60° V-tool
- Flexcut palm set and mini palm set
- Flexcut 1¼" carving knife
- Brushes (to apply lacquer and paint)

Carving a Santa in Motion

By John Zanzalari

While carving Santa figures is my hobby, doing so in a manner that implies a cold stormy Christmas Eve is my passion. This design was inspired by Victorian-era postcards depicting Santa Claus slowly making his way through forests of drifting snow during his annual Christmas Eve trek.

For this project I use a 4" x 8" x 10" block of tupelo. Ease of carving and the ability to hold detail are important considerations in the selection of wood, but I chose tupelo because light sanding quickly removes large quantities of unwanted material.

Carving Santa

Transfer the pattern onto the block of wood, then remove as much waste material as possible with a band saw. Use a rotary power carver outfitted with a tungsten carbide burr to refine the shape. Smooth the figure using a 120-grit sanding drum in the same tool. Carve the folds into the coat by holding the carbide burr vertically and pressing it deeply into the coat, leaving a deeper impression at the bottom of the coat than at the waist area. Complete each fold by using a carving knife to bring the top of each fold to a point. Use the same knife to add the hand, coat, and lantern details. Use a detail knife to carve the face. Add texture to the hair with a 4mm 60° V-tool.

Finishing Santa

Hand sand the entire figure lightly with 120-grit sandpaper. Then paint the carving with undiluted acrylic paint. Paint the face with flesh, and while the paint is still wet, apply a touch of cardinal crimson to each cheek and the tip of the nose. Blend the paints to achieve a light blush. Apply old Christmas red to the coat and vineyard green to the bag, the scarf, and the material on the staff. Apply titanium white to the beard, mustache, inside of the lantern, and the base. Leave the boots, mittens, staff, and rest of the lantern unpainted. When the paint has dried, apply a thin coat of clear acrylic sealer to the entire figure. When the sealer is dry, lightly sand the areas where there would be wear from years of handling. Mix equal parts dark brown antiquing medium and water. Apply the thinned solution to the entire carving with a 1"-wide China bristle brush. The thinned solution flows better into the grooves of the carving. Immediately wipe the carving down with dry cotton rags to remove the excess antiquing solution.

Allow the antiquing solution to dry for 30 minutes. Mix two parts titanium white with one part water. Dip a stiff-bristle toothbrush into the thinned paint and run your thumb deeply across the bristles four or five times into a paper towel to remove the excess paint. Then hold the toothbrush approximately 6" from the carving and run your thumb across the bristles to create a splatter of snow. This will take a bit of practice to produce small drops of paint. If the drops are too thick, remove them with a damp cloth.

materials & tools

MATERIALS:
- 4" x 8" x 10" block of tupelo
- ⅜"-diameter by 10"-long birch dowel (staff)
- Acrylic paints:
  Flesh
  Vineyard green
  Cardinal crimson
  Old Christmas red
  Titanium white
- Fabric-backed sandpaper, 120 grit
- Clear acrylic matte sealer
- Dark antiquing medium
- Cotton cloth
- Paper towel

TOOLS:
- Band saw
- Rotary power carver
- Tungston carbide bit of choice
- Sanding drum
- Carving knife
- Detail knife
- Pfeil palm-handled 4mm #2 bent V-tool
- 1"-wide China bristle brush
- #10 round brush
- #10 shader brush
- Hard-bristle toothbrush

Snowstorm Santa patterns

Patterns are drawn to scale on a 1" grid. Enlarge or reduce to desired size.

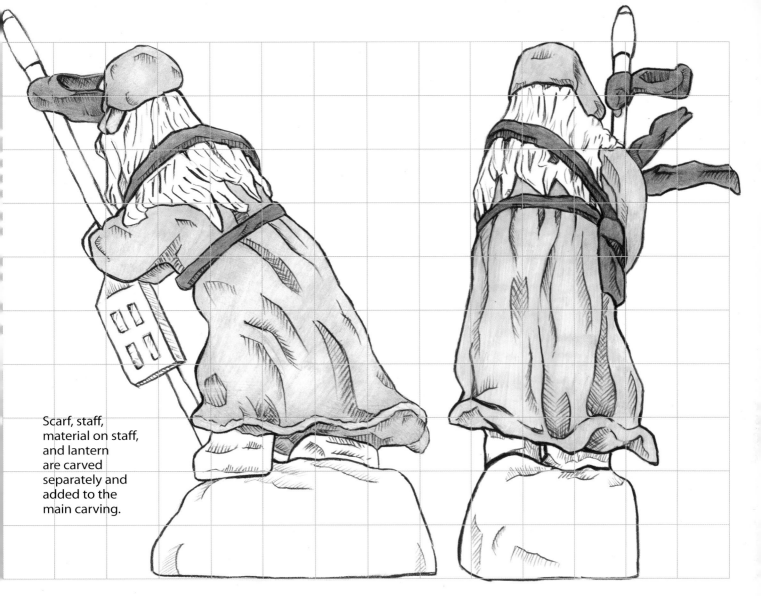

Scarf, staff, material on staff, and lantern are carved separately and added to the main carving.

JOHN'S FINISHING TIPS

tips

1. After removal of the antiquing solution, lighter colors may look dark or drab. You can remove additional antiquing solution with a damp cotton cloth.

2. When applying snow to a carving, the horizontal surfaces should receive more snow than the vertical surfaces.

3. The toothbrush method can be used to apply darker colors to represent age spots, to produce an older-looking finish.

Noah's Ark Santa

By Steve Brown

Santa Claus and Noah's Ark aren't a traditional pairing, but the two blend together nicely in this folk art carving. The relatively simple pose with hands tucked warmly into mittens makes the project accessible for less experienced carvers.

Santa, the tree, and the ark are all carved from a solid block of wood. I carve the animals separately and glue them into the pockets. I use a variety of hand tools on this fellow. Most of the carving is painted with acrylic paints thinned with water to the consistency of a wash. I use undiluted ultramarine and black for the eyes.

materials & tools

MATERIALS:
- 4" x 4" x 11½" basswood or wood of choice
- Acrylic paints:
  Navy blue (coat and pants)
  Golden brown (fur)
  Burnt umber (dry brush on fur, very thin wash for ark)
  Ultramarine (undiluted for iris)
  Black (undiluted for pupil, thinned for boots and gloves)
  Maroon (cheek and nose highlights)
  Dark forest (tree)
  Textured silver (tree highlights)
  Antique white (moustache, beard, and hair)
  White (beard and moustache highlights)

TOOLS:
- Palm-size V-tools: ⅟₁₆", ⅛", ⁵⁄₁₆"
- ³⁄₁₆" palm-size veiner
- ³⁄₁₆" #9 gouge
- Carving knife
- Carving glove
- Paintbrushes of choice

SPECIAL SOURCES
Noah's Ark Santa roughouts are available from *www.sbrownwoodcarving.com*, or 270-821-8774.

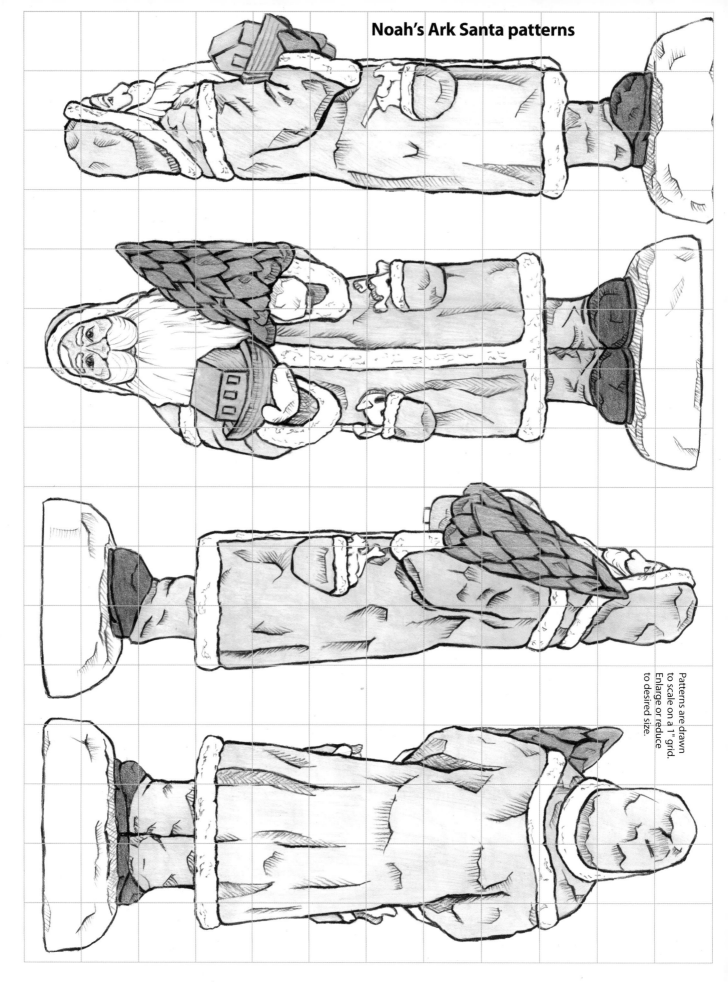

Patterns are drawn to scale on a 1" grid. Enlarge or reduce to desired size.

Weight Watcher Santa

By Arnold Smith

I was hesitant when originally asked to create a Santa carving. Most of my carvings have a unique perspective and I didn't want to carve the typical jolly round Kris Kringle. As I gave the project some more thought, I developed an image of Santa with a cinched-up belt showing off his newly svelte figure.

A skinny Santa is more difficult to carve than a traditional plump one. Some areas become fragile and require extra caution. The arm holding the staff is the weakest part of the carving due to the grain direction.

Cut the perimeter of the carving on a band saw, then drill the holes in the hands. The staff and two-part sack are add-ons. Use the photo as a guide and paint the carving with acrylic paint thinned with water. Use undiluted paint for the eyes and buttons.

materials & tools

MATERIALS:
- 4" x 5" x 12" basswood or wood of choice (Santa)
- 3" x 3" x 4" basswood or wood of choice (sack)
- ¼"-diameter by 4" dowel (staff)
- Acrylic paint:
  Tomato spice
  White
  Black
  Medium flesh
  Liberty blue
  Brown iron oxide
- Metallic 14K gold paint

TOOLS:
I prefer palm-size tools, but use your tools of choice
- ¹³⁄₁₆" #6 gouge
- ⁹⁄₁₆" #9 gouge
- #11 gouges: ⅛" and ¼"
- V-tools: 1mm, ¼"
- Bench knife
- Detail knife
- Paintbrushes of choice

Weight Watcher Santa patterns

Patterns are drawn to scale on a 1" grid. Enlarge or reduce to desired size.

Passing Preflight Inspection

By Sandy Smith

Sandy spent 138 hours on this carving. She kept track of the hours by making note of the times listed on audio books checked out from the library.

"Passing Preflight Inspection" was designed specifically for the 2008 *Woodcarving Illustrated* Santa Carving Contest. Trying to come up with an original idea for my contest entry was a huge challenge. Santa is a popular subject and has been portrayed in countless ways. I decided to pair Santa with Rudolph the red-nosed reindeer as a fawn. I've seen Rudolph carved as an adult many times, but I had never seen him carved as a fawn.

Sandy posed with her cocker spaniel, Charley, during the initial planning stages.

Planning the Carving

Our blonde cocker spaniel, Charley, seemed about the right size for modeling Rudolph as a fawn, so I had my husband take pictures of Charley and me from all angles. To get the proportions correct for Rudolph, I searched Google images web pages for photos of a sitting fawn, but did not find a single one. This led me to further research on fawns and their anatomy, where I learned that deer do not sit—especially in the position I had originally planned.

The pose I settled on was Santa checking Rudolph's red nose and Rudolph kissing Santa's nose. I know deer do not have lips that can pucker up for a kiss, but neither do they have noses that glow—I consider it artistic license.

I made armatures out of soft aluminum modeling wire using measurements from the reference photos and drawings. I added wood, crumpled-up aluminum foil, and duct tape to fill out the armatures and conserve clay. Armed with reference photos and materials, such as my husband's Marine Corps pilot's flight boots, I made a model out of clay.

Details were worked out in clay before Sandy took knife to wood.

Carving the Figures

Excluding the base, Santa and Rudolph were carved from a single piece of basswood. The blank was larger than my band saw could safely handle, so I used hand tools to rough out the carving. After drawing the front and side views on the basswood, I realized there was no way to clamp or secure the carving on a vise without leaving gaping holes that would later need to be filled.

I held the blank against a wood dog on my work bench or in my lap and started bringing my vision to life with reciprocating tools and then hand chisels. It was a tedious and time-consuming process that become a tad dangerous when I chiseled out wood between Santa and Rudolph's legs. Sometimes even carving gloves don't stop a sharp chisel.

Painting and Finishing

I paint my carvings with an acrylic paint wash to add subtle color while allowing the wood to show through. To make a paint wash, mix one drop of paint with 12 drops of water-based wood stain clear base tint. After the paint is dry, I seal my carvings with spray lacquer.

Santa's suit and hat were colored with washes of red apple and burgundy mixed for the reds, and white washes for the trim. I added shadows with a very small amount of navy blue acrylic paint and an acrylic blending gel. I painted Rudolph with a variety of tans, browns and whites, and used raw sienna for the shadows. Rudolph's nose is neon pink with a drop of pearl finish to give it a glow. The snow on the base is a combination of white and pearl-finish paints.

Texturing the Trim on Santa's Suit

Planning is an integral part of any original carving, but executing the details well is equally important. From the fur trim on Santa's suit down to the sole of his boots, the details are what brings a carving to life. If you are unfamiliar with creating any portion of your carving, practice on scrap wood to perfect your technique before attempting to create the effect on your carving.

1 **Rough out the shape.** Replicate the shape of the carving you want to texture. Adding texture to a flat piece of wood can be very different from texturing a rounded shape. Use a bench knife to round the wood to resemble a cylinder or, in this case, an arm.

2 **Add definition.** Shape the scrap wood to resemble the finished carving. Make a stop cut between Santa's sleeve and the fluffy trim with a knife or V-tool. Reduce the sleeve leaving the trim area larger than the sleeve to give the trim a fluffy appearance.

3 **Add rough texture.** It's often easier to create a realistic effect by working in stages. The first step for Santa's trim is to create the overall bunches and folds. I use a ⅜"-wide U-gouge. Use your tool of choice.

4 **Carve more details.** Working within the general contours created in step 3, add a second layer of finer details. Use a ⅛" or 3mm #11 gouge. Make a series of shallow cuts over the entire trim area.

5 **Woodburn additional texture.** Use a ball-tip woodburning pen to burn dimples in each gouge mark. Because the trim will be white, keep the temperature low. For fur or feathers, you may want a higher temperature.

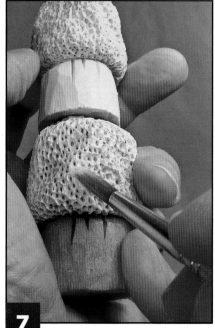

6 **Woodburn fine details.** A woodburner can often achieve more precise details than carving tools. Switch to a pin-point woodburning pen and burn a hole in each dimple. Fine woodburning tips are excellent for feather quills and fur texture, such as on Rudolph's coat.

7 **Paint the trim.** Use acrylic paint mixed with water-based wood stain clear tint base to produce a wash, which allows the wood grain to show through. For darker colors, apply additional coats. Dry brush the trim with a stiff brush and full-strength white acrylic paint to highlight the texture.

materials & tools

MATERIALS:
- Scrap basswood (to practice texturing)
- 6" x 9" x 10" basswood (Santa and Rudolph)
- 1¼" x 10" x 12" basswood (base)
- Acrylic paints:
  White
  Navy blue
  Red apple
  Burgundy
  Brown
  Tan
  Neon pink
- Pearl-finish paint
- Water-based stain clear tint base
- Spray lacquer

TOOLS:

I use a variety of tools. Use the tools you have available and with which you are most comfortable.

Texturing Tools:
- Carving knife
- ⅜"-wide U-gouge
- ⅛" or 3mm #11 gouge
- Woodburner with ball-tip and pin-point pens
- Paintbrushes of choice
- Stiff paintbrush (dry brushing)

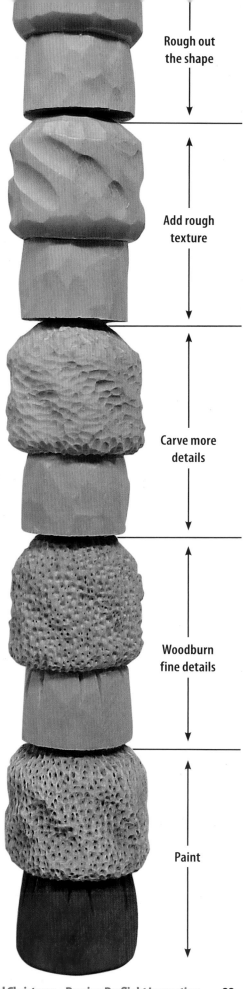

Rough out the shape

Add rough texture

Carve more details

Woodburn fine details

Paint

Preflight Inspection patterns

Patterns are drawn to scale on a 1" grid. Enlarge or reduce to desired size.

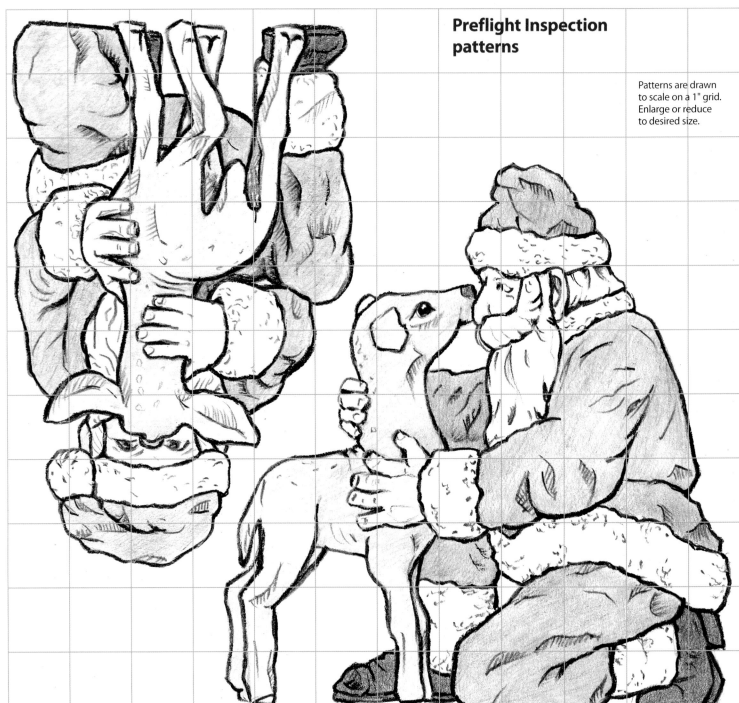

© 2011 Woodcarving Illustrated

Patterns are drawn
to scale on a 1" grid.
Enlarge or reduce
to desired size.

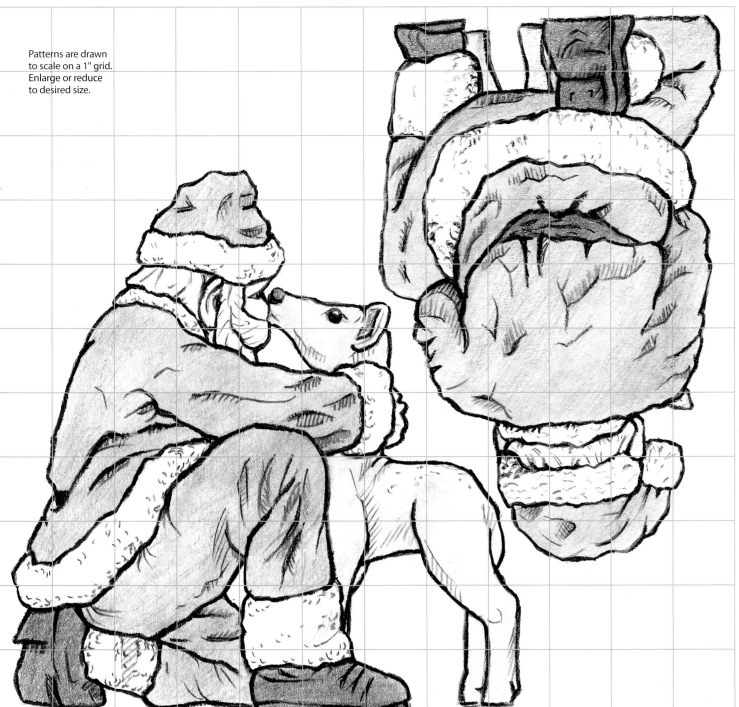

© 2011 Woodcarving Illustrated

Carve a Santa Egghead

By Rick Jensen

Commercially available basswood eggs make short work of the roughing-out process. You can quickly move on to blocking in the features and adding detail. With a little extra effort, these cheerful fellows can be carved from a block of basswood.

Beginners will get the best results by starting with a turned egg. The egg shape makes it easier to keep the carving symmetrical. Whether you start with an egg or block of wood, begin by transferring the pattern to the wood. Carve the general shape before adding any details or texture.

Painting the Egghead Santa

Paint the eyes first. Apply undiluted ivory to the entire eye. Paint the iris with liberty blue. Add a black pupil, then an ivory highlight in one corner of the pupil.

Mix boiled linseed oil (BLO) and a small amount of raw sienna together in a small jar. Paint the entire carving with this mixture. Add flesh oil paint to a little bit of the BLO mixture and apply it as a highlight to the cheeks, mouth, and nose.

Add titanium white to a bit of the original BLO mixture and apply it to the hair, beard, eyebrows, and ball on the hat. Paint the rest of the hat with alizarin crimson combined with the original BLO mixture.

Set the carving aside to dry or seal it right away with a few coats of semi-gloss lacquer.

materials & tools

MATERIALS:
- Ostrich-size basswood egg or 3" x 3" x 3¾" basswood
- Boiled linseed oil
- Oil paints:
  Raw sienna
  Alizarin crimson
  Flesh
  Titanium white
- Semi-gloss lacquer (optional)
- Acrylic paints (eyes):
  Ivory
  Liberty blue
  Black

TOOLS:
- Bench knife
- Large V-tool
- Small V-tool
- Assortment of veiners
- Assorted paintbrushes

Egghead Santa pattern

Photocopy at 100%

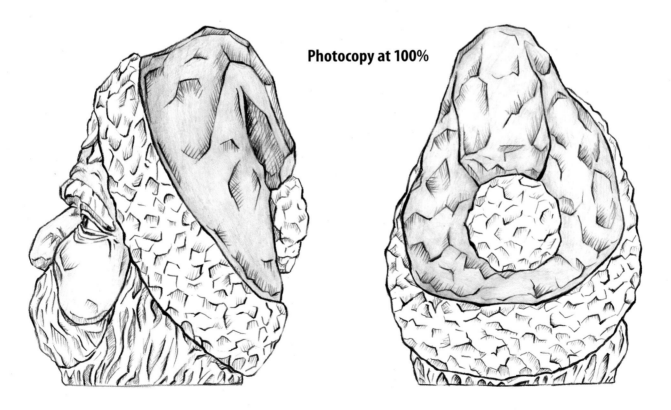

Photocopy at 100%

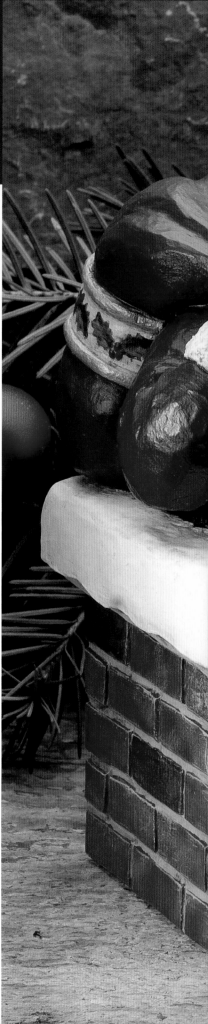

Gifts

The projects in this chapter are wonderfully decorative but also functional—which makes them perfect gifts. Simpler ones, such as the Santa pencils, are great day-brighteners for anyone who crosses your path. More involved ones, such as the Christmas puppy towel holder, serve as splendid thank-yous for those who host holiday gatherings. And at the larger end of the spectrum, a full-blown Santa candy dish or treasure box may be that perfect present you need for the really special people in your life. Or, of course, you could keep them for yourself—happy carving!

Secret Treasures Santa Claus,
by Deborah Call, page 138.

Whittling Santa Pencils

By Ron Johnson
Step-by-step photos by James A. Johnson

This quick-carve project is lots of fun and makes a perfect stocking stuffer. Santa's face is carved into an ordinary pencil—an affordable material readily found at dollar and discount stores.

My first exposure to carving pencils was in 2002 when a local carver named Elmer Sellers showed me how to carve a face in a standard pencil using only a knife. Since then, my carving technique has evolved, and I have given away hundreds of Santa pencils during the past six years.

Leave a Santa pencil with a tip at restaurants or give them to anyone who shows an interest. Carving pencils at a picnic table in a campground always brings interested visitors. The Santa pencils are a traditional Christmas treat for my granddaughter's teacher and classmates. Cut off the lower portion of the pencil and thread a string through the eraser for a unique Christmas ornament.

Carve printed pencils on the side opposite the printing or carve away the printing when you remove the paint. A good material source is a local supplier that imprints pencils for advertising. Buy the pencils without printing in your color of choice.

I use red hexagonal pencils to instantly convey Santa's red suit. Round pencils work just as well, but I suggest you use a hexagonal pencil for your first attempt. Use plain wooden pencils and leave them unpainted to represent wood spirits. You can also carve flat carpenter's pencils.

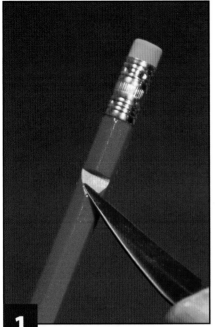

1 **Shape the forehead.** Use the ridge between two flat planes of the pencil as a centerline. Make a stop cut perpendicular to the ridge ½" down from the metal collar and as deep as the two adjacent ridges. Do not cut deep enough to hit pencil lead. Move down ³⁄₁₆" and cut up to the stop cut to remove a V-shaped chip.

2 **Remove the paint from the carving area.** Start about 2" below the stop cut made in step 1. Hold your knife at a low angle and slice the paint off the flat planes on either side of the centerline. It may take four or more slices to remove the paint. If your knife digs into the grain, start your cut from the other end.

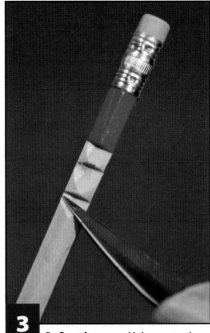

3 **Define the nose.** Make a second stop cut just below the start of the angled cut made in step 1. Move down ³⁄₁₆" and cut up to the stop cut to remove the chip. Move down ¼" from the second stop cut and make a third stop cut. Carve up to the third stop cut from ³⁄₁₆" below to remove a third chip.

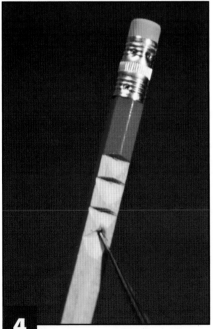

4 **Define the mustache.** Move down an additional ³⁄₁₆" and position the knife point on the centerline ridge. Make a cut at a 45° angle from the centerline down to the edge of the flat plane. Repeat for the other side of the mustache. Cut up from ³⁄₁₆" below the center of the mustache to remove the chip. Remove the centerline ridge from the mustache down to the painted area.

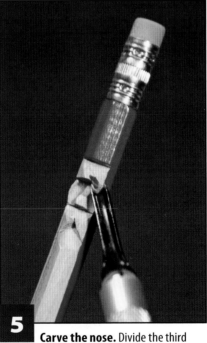

5 **Carve the nose.** Divide the third stop cut, just above the mustache, into thirds. Carve away the two outer thirds with a ⅛"-wide gouge. Angle the cuts toward the centerline slightly. Leave the center third as the nose. Varying the angle of these gouge cuts increases or decreases the width of the nose. Use a knife to free the chips if necessary.

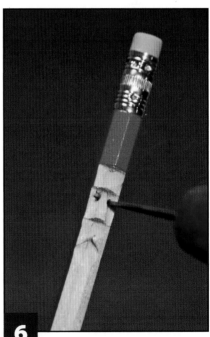

6 **Carve the eyes.** Stab the point of an old knife straight down, perpendicular to the pencil, at the top of the gouge cut made in step 5. Move it back and forth a few times to create the eye. Repeat the process for the other eye. Position the back side of the knife toward the nose to make symmetrical eyes.

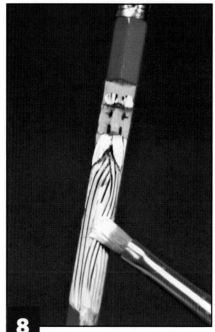

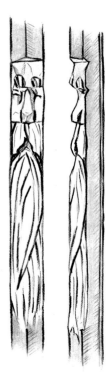

Santa pencil pattern

7 Woodburn the texture and shadows. Use a woodburner to add three short vertical lines for each eyebrow. Use the flat side of the burner to add a small shadow near the tip of both sides of the nose. Burn four curved lines on each side of the mustache. Add three more lines to define the bottom of the mustache. Then burn long flowing lines in the beard.

8 Paint the carving. Add a small dab of paint on each eyebrow and paint the mustache. Thin the paint for the beard so the burned detail shows through. Carve off a small area of paint on the back of the carving and sign and date your work. You may want to use initials to save space.

SAFE CARVING **tips**

Choose full-size pencils and hold the lower portion, well below the carving area, in your non-carving hand. Hold the upper part of the pencil on a flat hard surface for controlled safe cuts.

materials & tools

MATERIALS:
• Standard pencil
• Acrylic paints: white or off-white

TOOLS:
• Detail knife
• #11 gouge: ⅛" or 2mm
• Woodburner
• Old knife
• Small paintbrush of choice

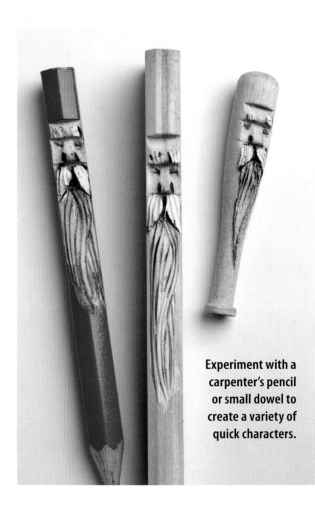

Experiment with a carpenter's pencil or small dowel to create a variety of quick characters.

Santa Earrings

By Rick Jensen

I hate throwing wood away and am always looking for ways to use my scraps. I designed these earrings to be carved from ¾" by ¾" stock. I carve an earring on each end of a 5"-long piece of wood so I have something to hold onto, but if you have a way to hold small pieces, you can get away with using two 2"- or 3"-long pieces.

Remove the corners of the ¾" by ¾" stock to turn it into a cylinder. Transfer the pattern to the blank and carve it to shape. The ball on Santa's hat is carved from a ⁵⁄₁₆"-square scrap of wood. Leave the bottom of the ball flat so you can attach it to the hat with cyanoacrylate (CA) glue. Paint the carving with acrylic paints, using whatever colors you want. When dry, apply a mixture of raw sienna oil paint and boiled linseed oil. Wipe off the excess oil and seal the carving with several coats of semi-gloss lacquer.

Attach the Earring Hooks
Instead of a screw eye, I use a #1 Aberdenn fishing hook. Cut off the bent part of the hook so you have a straight shank with an eye on the end. Use needle-nose pliers to push the shank into the top of the earring. If the shank is not secure in the Santa, use a dot of of CA glue. Attach an earring hook to the eye at the end of the shank. Earring hooks are available at most arts and crafts stores.

Earring patterns

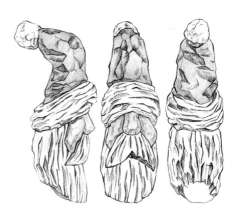

Photocopy at 100%

materials
& tools

MATERIALS:
- 2 each ¾" x ¾" x 2" or 1 each ¾" x ¾" x 5" basswood (earrings)
- 2 each ⁵⁄₁₆" x ⁵⁄₁₆" x ⁵⁄₁₆" basswood (hat ball)

- Acrylic paints:
  Tomato spice (hat)
  Red iron oxide (blush on cheeks and nose)
  Medium flesh (face)
  Ivory (beard, hat, hat trim)
- Boiled linseed oil

- Raw sienna oil paint
- Cyanoacrylate glue
- 2 each #1 Aberdenn fishing hooks (shanks)
- 2 each earring hooks

TOOLS:
- Knife of choice
- Small V-tool
- Paintbrushes of choice
- Needle-nose pliers with wire cutter

Christmas Puppy

By Sandy Smith

This cute little puppy nestled in a Christmas stocking is designed to hang on your towel rack and dress up your guest bathroom. The project can also be used without the hardware as an ornament for your Christmas tree.

To make a decorative towel bar accent, start with a commercial shower hook. The decorative portion of the shower hook should be about 1⅛" diameter. This provides the base to attach the carving. Cut off any overhanging parts and sand the base flat with a belt sander or rotary power carver. Be sure to wear eye protection!

Trace the outline of the pattern onto a basswood blank and cut it out with a scroll saw.

Determine the position of the shower curtain hanger on the back of the blank and mark the location of the hanger's base. Use a 1⅛"-diameter Forstner bit in a drill press to drill a ½"-deep hole. Do not glue the hanger in place yet.

Carve the puppy and stocking design on the front of the blank using your tools of choice. Paint the carving with acrylic paints. Allow the paint to dry and apply a neutral-color shoe polish.

Finally, attach the hanger to the back of the carving with two-part five-minute epoxy. If you will be using the carving as a Christmas tree ornament, insert a small eye hook in the corner of the stocking to suspend the ornament.

Puppy patterns

Photocopy at 100%

Reshape the decorative portion of the shower curtain hook with a belt sander or rotary carver.

materials
& tools

MATERIALS:
- 1¼" x 2½" x 4½" basswood or wood of choice
- 1⅛"-diameter decorative shower curtain hanger
- Two-part five-minute epoxy
- Acrylic paints of choice
- Neutral-color shoe polish

TOOLS:
- Carving knife of choice
- Assorted gouges and V-tools
- Rotary power carver and assorted bits
- Drill press with 1⅛"-diameter Forstner bit

Add some holiday cheer to your guest bathroom by using a shower curtain hook on the back of your carving.

Carve a Gift-Bearing Santa

By Don Dearolf
Process photos by Pete Kovarovic

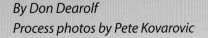

This little Santa was created with the thought of giving in mind. Instead of leaving a tip on the table for my favorite waiter or waitress, I carve a gift-bearing Santa and let him hand over the cash. Once the bill is removed, you can insert the candle from the backpack into Santa's hand.

Use this jolly little fellow to add a personal touch to any monetary gift. Tuck a larger bill in his hand and you have the perfect gift for the friend who has everything. Replace the rolled-up bill with a personal note for a Christmas gift that will be cherished for years to come.

Best of all, you can complete the entire carving with a single knife, he's easy to paint, and you don't have to carve eyes! Transfer the pattern to the blank and cut out the shape with a band saw. Drill a ¼"-diameter hole through the hand and a ¼"-diameter by ½"-deep hole in the backpack.

Personalize your Santa by changing the beard or hat, or get creative for year-round fun.

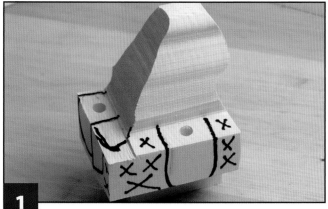

1 **Draw the backpack and mitten.** Mark the center of the hole in the backpack and make a mark ½" from the centerline on both sides to represent the sides of the backpack. Then draw in the mitten and mark the waste wood.

2 **Remove the waste and round the corners.** Remove the extra wood around the mitten and backpack. Remove the sharp corners and saw marks from the entire figure. Round and shape the arm, mitten, and backpack.

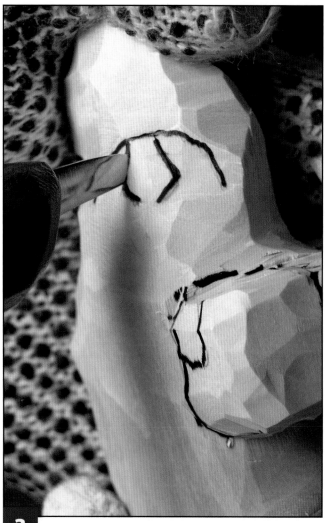

3 **Establish landmarks for the face.** Rough in the face mound and draw the nose, which is just right of center. Sketch the bottom of the hood. Plunge your knife in to make stop cuts just outside of the lines for the nose. Do not make a stop cut at the bottom of the nose because this areas will be slanted down toward the mustache.

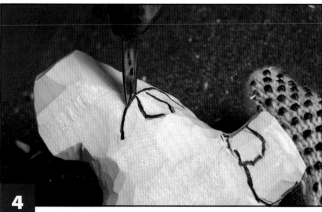

4 **Carve the hood.** Shape the hood and tassel, which narrow toward the back. Plunge your knife in, making a stop cut along the inside of the line for the bottom of the hood. Start at the outside corner of the eye channel. Carve in deep on both sides of the nose. Keep the knife pointed slightly downward.

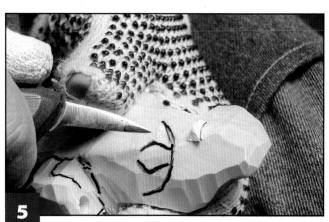

5 **Carve the eye channels and cheeks.** Cut from the outside corner of the hood to the wing of the nose, above what will be the nostril. Remove the triangular chips of wood to make the eye channels and the cheeks.

6 **Finish shaping the nose.** Make two angled cuts under the nose to define the tip of the nose and the top of the mustache. Sketch in the mustache and carve up to the wings of the nose to separate the nose from the cheeks.

7 **Carve the mustache.** Make stop cuts on the mustache lines. Then cut down slightly along the top of the mustache to separate the cheeks. Cut up at a slight angle along the bottom of the mustache to separate the mustache from the beard.

8 **Carve the hand and arms.** Mark and carve the hand wearing the mitten. Undercut the thumb. Remove the wood on the shoulders on the front and back of both arms

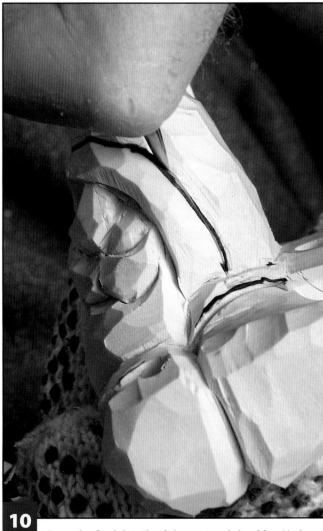

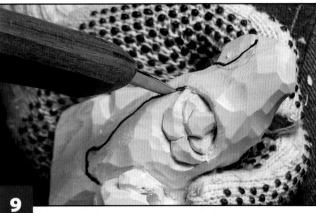

9 **Outline the beard and hood tassel.** Sketch in the beard and tassel. Make a deep stop cut all the way around the beard. Then cut from outside the line down to the bottom of the stop cut. This will make the beard stand out. Use the same technique to outline the tassel.

10 **Carve the final details of the coat and shoulder.** Mark the fur line and shoulder straps. Make a stop cut all the way around the fur line of the hood. Carve down from above to this stop cut to expose the fur line. Then carve in the shoulder straps.

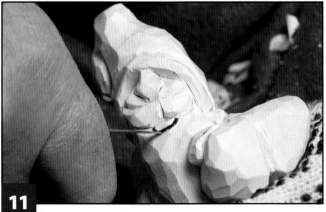

11 **Carve the bottom lip.** Mark the lip and make a stop cut on the line. Cut up to the stop cut from below, making a slight undercut to form the lip. Sketch in the lines of Santa's coat.

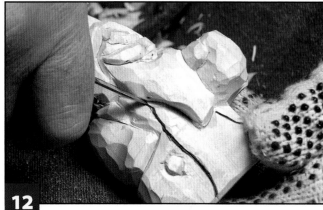

12 **Carve Santa's coat.** Make deep stop cuts straight in along the coat lines. Cut from inside the lines up to the stop cut and relieve the robe area. Carve the button.

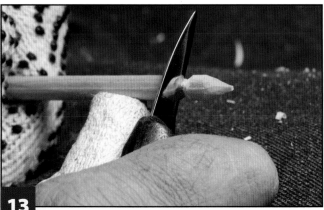

13 **Carve the candle.** Use a 6"-long piece of ¼"-diameter dowel. Make a stop cut ½" in from the end of the dowel. This is the bottom of the flame. Shape the flame and cut the candle to a final length of about 2". Seal the candle with matte finish, paint with thinned acrylic paint, and then apply another coat of matte finish.

14 **Finish the carving.** Seal the carving with a light coat of matte spray finish. When dry, paint the carving with several layers of acrylic paint thinned heavily with water. Dry brush a very light coat of white over the carving to make the facets stand out. Allow the paint to dry and apply another coat of matte finish.

materials & tools

MATERIALS:
- 2" x 3¼" x 4¼" basswood or wood of choice
- ¼"-diameter by 6"-long dowel
- Acrylic paints of choice
- Matte spray finish

TOOLS:
- Carving knife of choice
- Drill with ¼"-diameter drill bit

Gift-Bearing Santa patterns

Photocopy at 100%

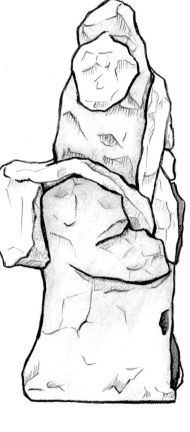

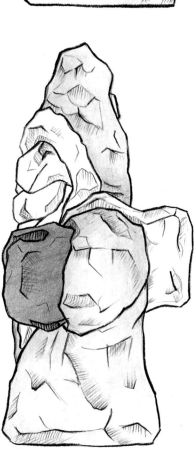

Folk Art Angel Tree Topper

By Shawn Cipa

This tree topper is an easy project that combines relief and in-the-round techniques. The stylized angel will fit in well with a wide array of holiday decorating styles. It uses the basic principles of relief carving, but it has carvings on both sides of the piece.

This is a conscious design choice that allows me to achieve the size I want without being so heavy that it bows the tree.

Carving the angel is a good lesson in stylized form and dealing with ever-changing grain direction. Since both sides are carved, the edges of the piece must tie the two sides together. I use several gouges to rough out the carving, but most of the details and final tweaks are done with a knife. I clamp the blank down during the roughing-out stage to provide control and to ensure safety.

Choose a clear piece of basswood for this project for both ease of carving and for painting purposes. Enlarge the pattern on a copier at 150%, cut it out, and trace it onto the blank. You can carve a smaller version, but it must be large enough to attract attention on top of your Christmas tree. You can also reduce the pattern for use as an ornament or carve one much bigger for those two-story trees!

After tracing the pattern onto the blank, cut it out. A scroll saw works best, because it lets you make the inside cut beneath the angel's lower arm. It also leaves a smooth cut.

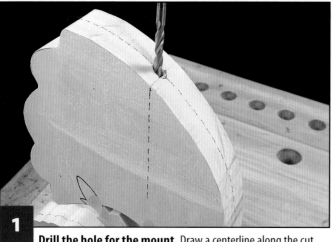

1 **Drill the hole for the mount.** Draw a centerline along the cut edge. Using the centerline and the guide on the pattern, drill a ¼"-diameter hole for the mount a few inches deep. Be sure to keep in line with the guides.

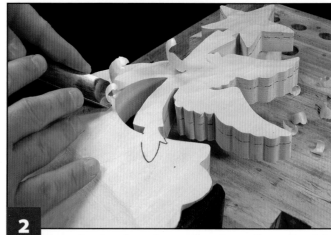

2 **Taper the piece from the angel's waist up.** Use a 1½" shallow gouge. Taper it down so the wood is about ¼" above the centerline near the star.

3 **Re-draw the shape of the lower hand.** Use a knife to trace the lower hand with deep, straight stop cuts. Using a ¾" fishtail gouge, begin rounding the inner curve of her robe—round to the centerline on the edges. This will define the lower hand as the wood is removed.

4 **Round the outer edge of the angel's robe.** Use the technique explained above. Work toward the middle, and give the robe a nice, tooled surface with a ¾" fishtail gouge. Use a knife to clean up the areas you can't get with the gouge for both the inner and outer curves of the robe.

5 **Make deep stop cuts around the head.** This separates the head from the wings and arms. I use a pelican-shaped blade, which makes the curved plunge cut easier.

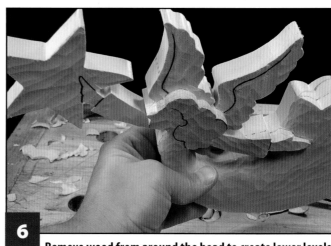

6 **Remove wood from around the head to create lower levels.** Taper the lower arm upward and "behind" her hair. Use a ½" fishtail gouge for the wood removal, and use a knife to keep the edges crisp.

7 Rough out the back side. Draw on the wing lines, and make stop cuts along the lines with a pelican-shaped knife. Then remove the wood from around them. Remove wood from the upper arm and star using a ½" fishtail gouge and a knife. The star should be no less than ¼" thick.

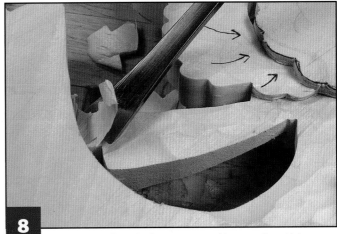

8 Taper and define the lower arm and lower wing. Make stop cuts to define the lower wing and the lower arm and remove wood up to these cuts using a ½" fishtail gouge and a knife to create separate levels.

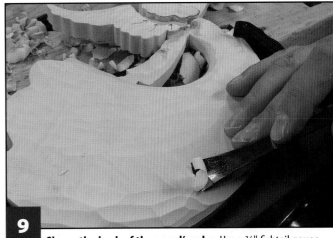

9 Shape the back of the angel's robe. Use a ¾" fishtail gouge and the same techniques you used on the front of the carving to round the backside of the robe to the centerline. Leave definite tool marks on the robe to create the folk art look.

10 Define the wings and hand on the back of the carving. Use stop cuts and undercutting to shape and define the levels for the wings, hand holding the star, and the sleeves of the robe. Use both a ½" fishtail gouge and a knife for this rounding and shaping process.

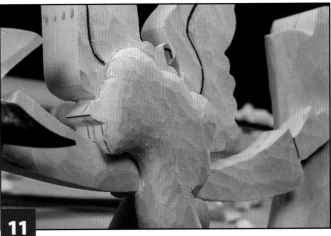

11 Round the head area. Use your knife of choice. Locate the centerline for her face, and narrow out the profile, bringing the nose to a point. On the back side, use the knife to separate the face from the upper arm and wing and further define the levels.

12 **Shape the wings.** You will be making concave and convex forms, using a ½" fishtail gouge. The right wing is cupped from the front, while the left wing is cupped from the back. Use a knife to keep it clean.

13 **Add the feathers.** Draw in the feather lines on the concave side only, for both the front and the back. Define these lines by tracing with a ⅜" V-tool tilted slightly on its side.

14 **Shape the lower arm.** Use a knife to round the arm and shape the hand. Notice how the hand rests on the front of the robe—be sure to keep it attached for strength.

15 **Shape the upper arm and star.** Use a knife. Notice the gripping hand and its relationship to the other side. When thinning the star, be careful; the arm has become fragile. Don't make anything less than ¼"-thick.

16 **Add the hairline.** Re-draw the hairline, and trace along it with a ⅛" V-tool or detail knife. You want to give separation to these areas, but do not carve too deeply. Keep in mind that her ear is over her hair, yet the lower hanging hair is over her neck.

17 **Shape the face and hair.** Sketch in the curls, and trace along the lines with a ⅛" V-tool. Use a detail knife to give the hair and face a final shaping and give definition to the chin area. The eye is a small, curved chip-cut made with a detail knife. Hollow the ear slightly.

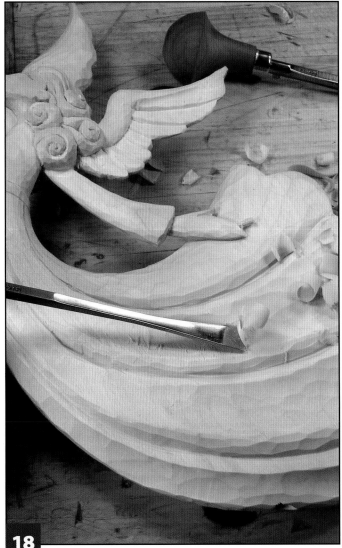

Finishing Notes

Start with a coat of boiled linseed oil and mineral spirits, mixed at 50/50. Wipe off the excess, and let it sit overnight. Then begin painting with matte craft acrylic paints. Keep the paints thinned with water, and apply the colors in layers. You may choose my colors or create your own scheme to match your tree's decorations. I use a lot of bright gold so that lights can reflect in the gold paint's surface—apply the gold at full strength. After the paint has dried, seal it with one good coat of spray or brush-on satin lacquer. When the lacquer has cured, antique the carving by slathering on a dark brown gel stain. Immediately wipe the carving clean of excess stain.

The tree mount

The mount is made from a length of #6 gauge copper ground wire available at most hardware stores. It is roughly ¼" thick and is quite sturdy, yet it is bendable. To achieve the shape, wrap it around a 1¼"-diameter dowel rod clamped in a vise. Wrap it evenly to make four or five coils; cut the excess with a hacksaw. Glue the straight end into the drilled hole, using a strong all-purpose cement.

18 **Shape the waistline and belt.** Use your knife of choice. Texture the robe, using the pattern as a guide. Sketch in some robe lines and trench out valleys along the lines with a ⅜" V-tool. Scallop out each area with a ½" fishtail gouge. Complete both sides.

19 **Hollow out the rear opening of the robe.** Use a ⅜" veiner. Attach the angel to the mount to aid in the finishing process.

materials & tools

MATERIALS:
- 1¼" x 7" x 14 " basswood blank
- 30" #6 gauge copper ground wire
- All-purpose cement

FINISHING MATERIALS:
- 50/50 mix of boiled linseed oil and mineral spirits
- Assorted paintbrushes
- Acrylic paints:
  Light blue (robe)
  Antique white (robe)
  Midnite blue (robe)
  Schoolbus yellow (hair and face)
  Tangerine (hair and face)
  Bright red (hair and face)
  Flesh (hair and face)
  Wicker white (wings)
  Pansy lavender (wings)
  Metallic splendid gold (wings)
- Satin lacquer (brush-on or spray)
- Brown, oil-based gel stain

TOOLS:
- Scroll saw or band saw (optional)
- Standard carving knife of choice
- Detail knife or pelican knife
- 1½" shallow gouge
- ¾" fishtail gouge
- ½" fishtail gouge
- ⅜" veiner
- ⅜" V-tool
- ⅛" V-tool
- Drill with ¼"-diameter bit
- Hacksaw

@SCIPA 2006

Holiday Memories
Santa

By Shawn Cipa

This Santa project provides an ideal way to display your favorite holiday photo. It also makes a great gift for family and friends. The folk-style photo holder is an easy and fun-to-do design that is perfect for beginners, and is a great break from involved projects that more experienced carvers may be working on.

The design is a very basic shape; it can be carved simply, or details may be added according to your skill level. For example, I have left the robe simple, but you may decide to add texture, folds, or ruffles. The tree pot could be carved as a more elaborately-shaped vessel. Alternatively, you could choose to omit the beard details for a simple, smooth effect.

I use several gouges to rough out the basic elements and to add details, but a knife could be used for most, if not all, of the work. Choose a clear piece of basswood for both ease of carving and painting purposes. Clamp the blank down during the roughing-out stage to provide control and ensure safety.

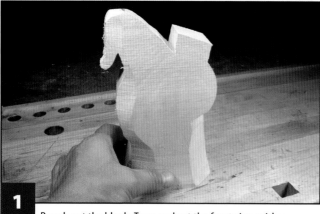

1 Rough out the blank. Trace and cut the front view with a band saw. There is no side-view pattern; simply cut a gentle taper from the bottom to the top. You can round the corners by hand, but to save time, I set the band saw table to cut at a 45°-angle and trim the waste off the corners.

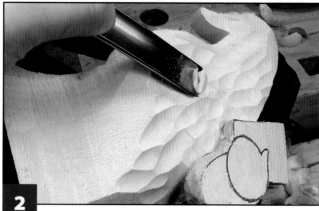

2 Define the left arm, glove, and the tree pot section. Transfer these details from the pattern to the blank. Make stop cuts along these lines with a knife. Taper the chest area so that the arm, glove, and pot are approximately ⅝" above the neck and belly. Use a ¾" shallow gouge or a carving knife.

3 Shape the right arm. Round the right arm with a ¾" shallow gouge. Draw in the right arm and glove. Make a stop cut around the arm and glove with a knife, and relieve up to the arm with the same gouge. This arm and glove should be approximately ½" above the chest.

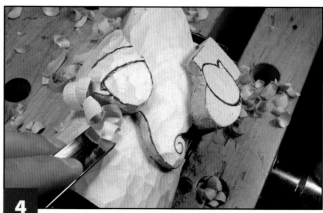

4 Shape the chest and beard. Round and shape the chest area between the arms. Draw in the beard. Make a stop cut along the beard with a carving knife. Taper and round the robe up to the stop cuts with a knife or a ¾" shallow gouge. The beard protrudes approximately ½" at its highest point.

5 Define the sections of the back. Sketch in the main sections. Make a V-cut along these lines with a ½" V-tool or a carving knife. Round and shape the back with a ¾" shallow gouge. The robe is tapered, the arms are rounded, the hood is rounded and tapered, and the tree pot is separated from the arm.

6 Add the details to the right arm. Draw in the cuff and the glove. Make a stop cut on both sides of the cuff. Shave away from the arm and glove up to the stop cuts on both sides of the cuff. Taper the glove so that it appears to protrude from inside the cuff. The cuff disappears beneath the glove where it meets the torso.

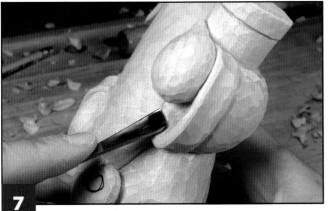

7 Shape the left arm. Remove wood from the left sleeve and the tree pot with a knife so the glove protrudes the most. Shape the glove, sleeve and tree pot with a knife. Sketch in the rim of the pot and the outer cuff. Make stop cuts and relieve around these elements. Sketch in the hollow below the glove, and scallop out the area with a ½" shallow fishtail gouge.

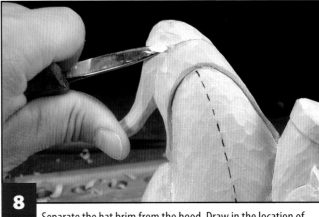

8 Separate the hat brim from the hood. Draw in the location of the hat brim. Make a stop cut with a knife above and below the brim. Taper the hood up to the stop cut. Remove a little wood from the forehead area to lay the groundwork for the facial area. Sketch in the centerline of the face to help orient the facial features. The center of the nose will be on the centerline.

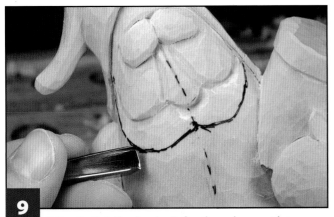

9 Define the facial landmarks. Define the eyebrows with a knife. Draw in the nose and cheeks. Follow along these lines with a ⅜" V-tool, and draw in the guidelines for the mustache. Use the centerline to keep all of the facial features symmetrical.

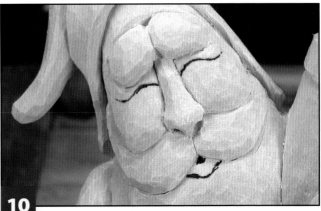

10 Add the nose, cheek, and mustache details. Carve the nostril holes and the open mouth with the tip of a knife. Draw in the guidelines for the upper eyelids and the lower lip. Taper the wood of the chin and beard away from the lower lip with a knife.

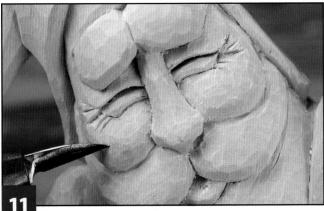

11 Add the eye details. Carve deep slits along the guidelines for the upper eyelids with a detail knife. Deepen the pockets just under the eyebrows. Draw in the lower eyelid bags, and shape them with a detail knife. Add crow's feet around the outer corners of each eye. These details help to increase the smiling effect.

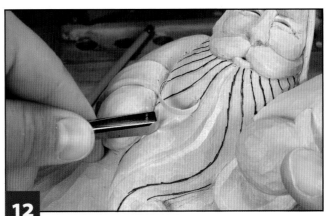

12 Add the beard details. Draw in flow guidelines. Carve along these lines with a ⅜" V-tool. Shape the "curly-cue" tip. Use a ⅛" V-tool to further detail the beard. Use the same technique to detail the mustache and eyebrows. Drill a ⅛"-diameter hole in the top center of the tree pot for the wire tree (see sidebar).

Finishing notes

Seal the carving with a mixture of equal parts boiled linseed oil and mineral spirits. Wipe off the excess, and allow the carving to dry overnight. Thin matte acrylic craft paints with water, and apply the colors in layers. You can use my carving as a guide or create your own color scheme.

After the paint has dried, seal it with one good coat of satin lacquer or a few thinned coats of polyurethane. When the clear coat has cured, antique the carving. Slather on a brown gel stain, and immediately wipe the excess stain off of the carving.

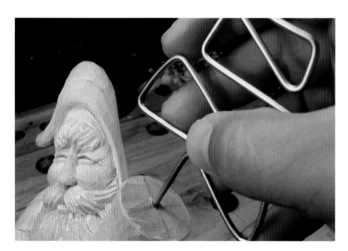

The Photo Holder

The holder is made from a common coat hanger wire. Use the thinnest gauge wire you can find. Cut the wire to length with snips. Sand off the glaze coating on the wire to prepare it for painting. Using one or two pairs of pliers, carefully bend it to shape according to the provided pattern. Paint the completed holder with high-gloss gold enamel spray paint. Once the paint has cured, mount it to the carving by gluing the stem into the drilled hole with cyanoacrylate (CA) glue or an all-purpose cement.

An interactive 3-D model of this carving may be seen here: *www.woodcarvingillustrated.com/ features/holiday-memories-santa.html*.

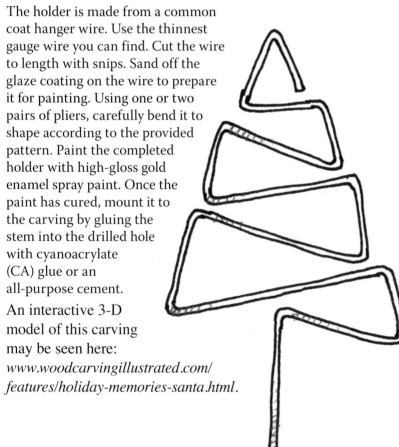

MATERIALS:

- 3" x 4½" x 7" basswood
- 18" of coat hanger wire
- Cyanoacrylate glue

FINISHING MATERIALS:

- 50/50 mix of boiled linseed oil and mineral spirits
- Assorted paint brushes
- Acrylic paints:
  Robe
  Bright red
  Royal purple (for shading)
  Summer lilac
  White
  Italian Sage (cuff shading)
  Gloves
  Hauser light green
  Black forest green
  School bus yellow
  Tangerine
  Face / Beard
  Flesh
  Bright red
  Antique white
  Light blue

Tree Pot
Terra cotta
Antique white

- Satin Lacquer or thinned polyurethane
- Brown, oil-based gel stain
- High-gloss gold enamel spray paint

TOOLS:

- Band saw (optional)
- Carving knife
- Detail knife
- ¾" shallow gouge
- ½" V-tool
- ½" fishtail gouge
- ⅜" V-tool
- ⅛" V-tool
- Drill with ⅛"-diameter bit
- Wire snips
- Pliers for bending
- Medium-grit sandpaper (to remove glaze from wire)

Photocopy at 100%

Holiday memories
Santa pattern

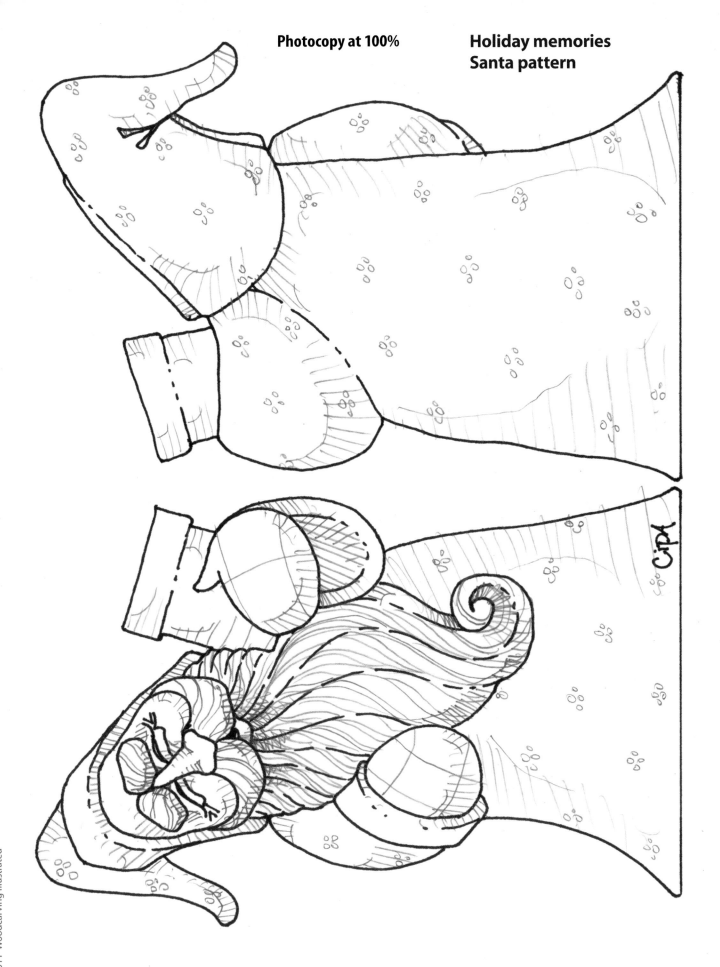

Whimsical Santa Holds Your Christmas Stocking

By Shawn Cipa

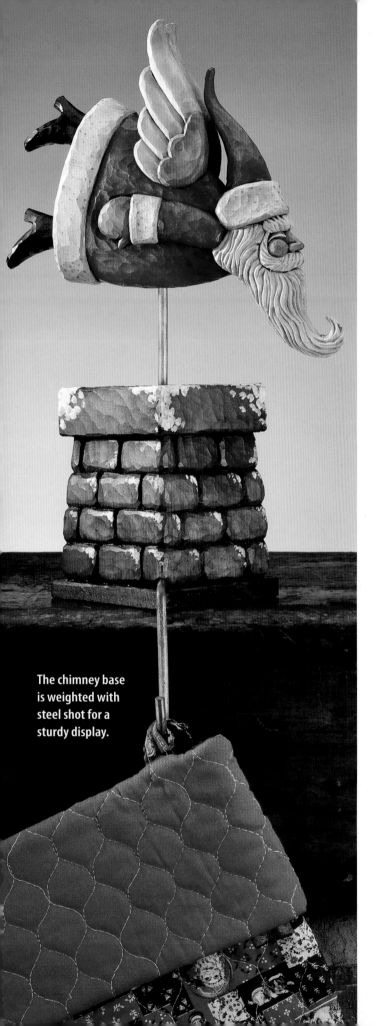

The chimney base is weighted with steel shot for a sturdy display.

This Santa angel is a charming way to display Christmas stockings. The base is hollowed and weighted with steel shot, providing the stability needed to support a stocking stuffed with holiday cheer. Carve one for each member in your family and personalize them with different paint schemes. Line the Santas on your mantel for a festive holiday display.

The Santa is carved from 2"-thick stock and combines elements of both in-the-round and relief carving. You can purchase inexpensive steel (or lead) shot at any sporting goods store. When completed, the entire project weighs about three pounds, which is more than enough to hold a filled stocking. I suggest not gluing the Santa onto the copper wire mount. This way, you can adjust the position of the Santa once the holder is in place, and it comes apart for easy storage.

Choose a clear piece of basswood for both ease of carving and painting purposes. Clamp the blank down during the roughing-out stage to provide control and ensure safety. Afterward, the Santa can be held in your hand as you add the details. The chimney base must be clamped in place when you hollow it out.

Stocking Holder: Bending the Wire

The hanger is made from a 15" length of #6 gauge copper ground wire, commonly found in any hardware store. It is roughly ³⁄₁₆" thick. The wire is sturdy but easy to bend. Cut it to length with a hacksaw and grind or hand-file the ragged ends smooth. To achieve the proper shape, you will need good pliers. A machine vise helps to work out the 90° angles. You may need to gently tap the piece with a hammer to keep it flat when lying on its side. The wire is not glued to the base; once it is in position, the steel shot combined with the construction adhesive and base plate will make it solid.

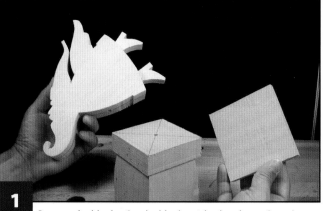

1 Prepare the blanks. Cut the blanks with a band saw. Santa's feet are ½" thick centered across the width of the blank. Drill ³⁄₁₆"-diameter holes in Santa's belly and the center top of the chimney base using the pattern as a guide. Draw a centerline around the perimeter of the Santa blank.

2 Round the Santa. Clamp the blank securely. I use an ordinary shop clamp gripped in my bench vise. Use a shallow 1¼"-wide gouge to round the head, beard, hat, and front of Santa's body. Work on one side of Santa, carving toward the centerline. Do not cross the centerline.

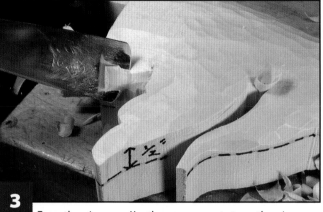

3 Taper the wing area. Use the same gouge to taper the wing until it is about ½" from the centerline. Round the robe area behind the wing. Flip the blank and repeat steps 2 and 3 on the opposite side. Draw the wings, arms, and fur trim on the hat and bottom of the robe using the pattern as a guide.

4 Define the elements. With the carving secured, outline the arm, wing, and fur trim on the hat and robe with a ½"-wide V-tool. Relieve about ⅛" of wood around these elements. Draw the feather details on the wing and the fur trim on the sleeve. Flip the carving and repeat the process on the opposite side.

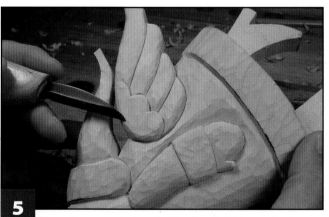

5 Shape the arm and wing. At this point, I hold the carving in my hand and carve with a knife. Separate and round the feathers in the wing. Round the arm and separate the fur cuff. The cuff should be slightly higher than the arm and mitten. Carve both sides using the same techniques.

6 Shape the face, beard, and hat. Use a carving knife. Remove the saw marks and round the corners of the face, beard, and hat. Taper the hat and beard to a blunt point. The hat trim is slightly higher than the hat. Thin the nose on both sides to form an edge at the centerline.

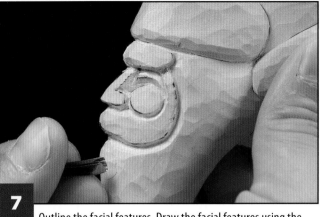

7 Outline the facial features. Draw the facial features using the pattern as a guide. Trace along the lines of the facial features with a ⅛"-wide V-tool. Outline the features on both sides.

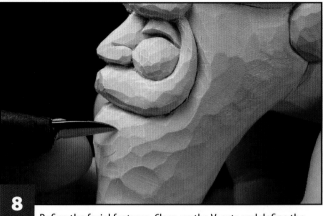

8 Refine the facial features. Clean up the V-cuts and define the eyebrow, cheek, eyelid, nose, and mustache with a small detail knife. Carve both sides and join the cuts together at the centerline.

9 Add texture to the hair, beard, and mustache. Use a V-tool or a macaroni tool to carve intersecting grooves on the beard, mustache, and eyebrows. Do not carve straight grooves. These grooves should be curved and flowing.

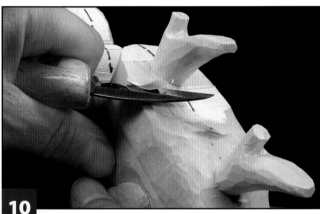

10 Carve the boots and bottom of the robe. Use a carving knife to shape the boots. Remove all the saw marks and round the edges on the fur trim at the bottom of the robe. The facets you are creating add to the folk-art feel of the project.

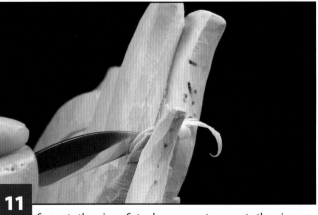

11 Separate the wings. Cut a deep groove to separate the wings on both the front and back. This will take several cuts. Be careful when cutting behind the fragile tip of the hat. Use a knife to clean up any rough areas on the entire carving. Use a ½"-wide fishtail gouge for tight spots.

12 Hollow the chimney. Clamp the blank upside down and drill five 1"-diameter by 3"-deep holes. Remove the wood between the holes with a shallow 1"-wide gouge and a mallet. Do not carve deeper than 3". The hole doesn't have to be perfect because it will not be visible in the completed carving.

13 Carve the bricks. Draw the bricks using the pattern as a guide. Trace along the lines with a ½"-wide V-tool. Refine the bricks with a carving knife. You can see several phases of completion in the photo. Carve all four sides, taking care to align the bricks at the corners.

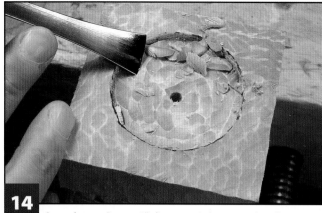

14 Carve the top. Draw a 2"-diameter circle centered on the ³⁄₁₆"-diameter hole. Stop-cut around the edge of the circle with a knife. Remove a little wood from inside the circle with a ¾"-wide fishtail gouge to simulate a chimney opening. Carve away the saw marks from the top of the chimney.

15 Carve the base of the chimney. Carve away the saw marks, working in approximately ½" from all of the edges and along all four sides. Use a fishtail gouge. Clean up and slightly round the corners with a knife.

16 Add the hanger and weight. Carve a small trench in the bottom corner of the chimney for the wire. Insert the pre-bent wire hanger, threading it up through the top of the chimney. Pour the shot into the cavity, leaving a ¼"-deep gap.

17 Seal the weight. Fill the gap with construction adhesive. Spread the adhesive out with a craft stick. Make sure the adhesive seals the corner where the copper wire rests to lock the wire in place.

18 Attach the base. Center the base on the bottom of the chimney, over top of the construction adhesive. The carved edges should face the bricks. Nail the base to the bricks using small finishing nails.

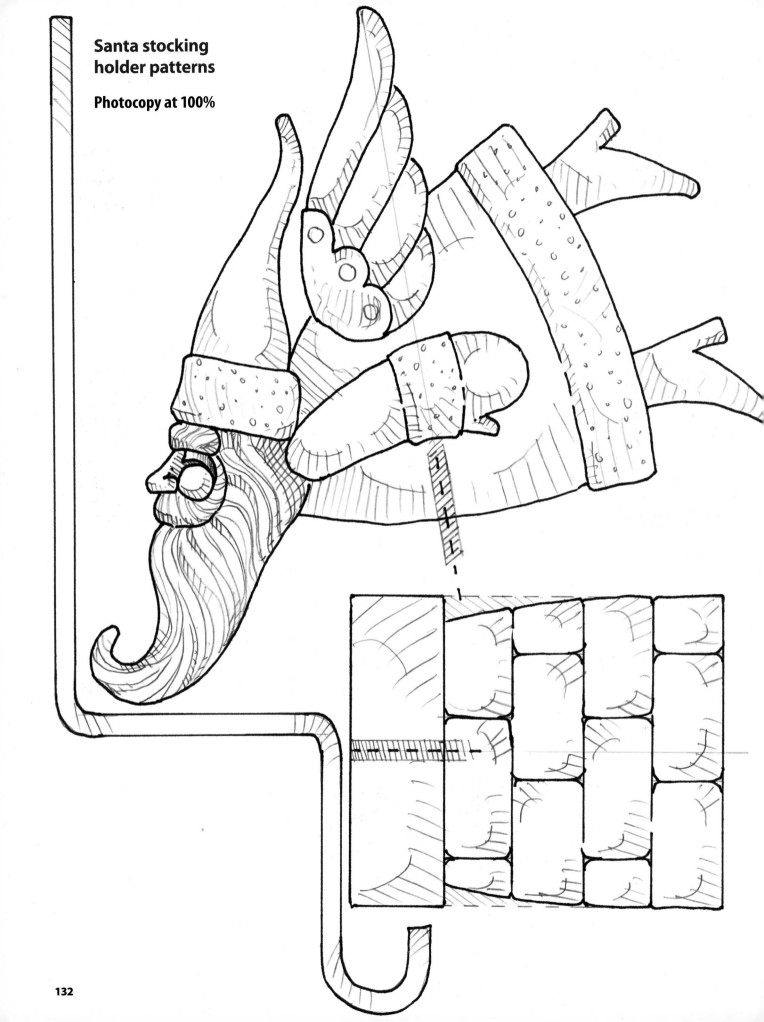

Santa stocking holder patterns

Photocopy at 100%

Coat the carving with a mixture of equal parts boiled linseed oil and mineral spirits. Wipe off the excess and let it dry overnight. Dispose of the oily rags properly. When the carving is dry, paint it with matte craft acrylic paints. Thin the paints with water and apply the colors in layers. Use the reference photos or develop your own color scheme. After the paint has dried, seal the carving with one good coat of satin lacquer or a few thinned coats of polyurethane. When the clear coat has cured, antique the carving by slathering on your brown gel stain of choice. Immediately wipe the excess stain off the carving.

MATERIALS:

- 2" x 6" x 8" basswood (Santa)
- 3¼" x 3¼" x 4" basswood (chimney)
- ¼" x 3½" x 3½" basswood (chimney base)
- 15" of #6 gauge copper ground wire
- 3 pounds of steel or lead shot
- General purpose construction adhesive
- 4 each small finishing nails
- Craft stick (for spreading adhesive)

FINISHING MATERIALS:

- 50/50 mix of boiled linseed oil and mineral spirits
- Satin lacquer or thinned polyurethane
- Brown oil-based gel stain
- Acrylic paints:
  Tuscan red (robe)
  Black (boots, chimney base)
  Splendid gold (fir trim, boots)
  Hauser light green (gloves)
  Black Forest green (gloves)
  Neutral gray (chimney base)
  Snow white (chimney base, beard)
  Primary red (tint natural wood on face)
  Antique white (fur trim, wings)
  Summer lilac (wings)
  Pansy lavender (wings)
  Boysenberry pink (wings)
  Barn red (chimney base)
  Raw sienna (fur trim shading)
  Light blue (beard shading)
  Tapestry wine (robe shading)

TOOLS:

- Band saw
- Carving knife of your choice
- Detail knife
- 1½"-wide shallow gouge
- ½"- and ⅛"-wide V-tool
- ½"-wide macaroni tool (optional)
- ½"- and ¾"-wide fishtail gouge
- 1"-wide shallow gouge
- Mallet
- Drill with ³⁄₁₆"-and 1"-diameter bits
- Assorted paintbrushes
- Hacksaw (to cut wire)
- Pliers (to bend wire)
- Hammer (to bend wire)
- Vise
- File or grinder (to smooth wire)

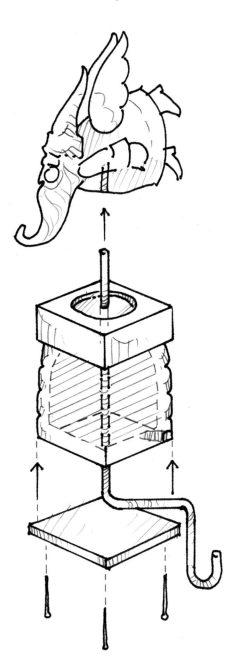

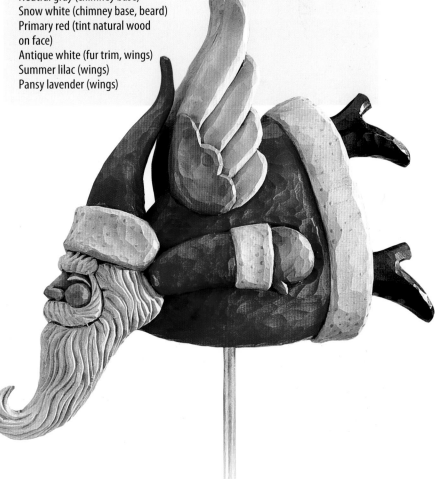

Carve a Christmas

By Jim McGuire

I created this festive candy dish with inspiration from a homeless person's "will work for food" sign and the time I spent living in Hershey, Pa., the chocolate capital of the world.

Carving the Santa

Start with a 4" x 7" x 12" piece of basswood. Cut the front profile and glue a 1" x 3" x 3" piece of wood onto the back for the backpack.

Use your tools of choice to carve the piece. Try to create a clean tooled finish on every surface. No fuzz is allowed—I don't use sandpaper on basswood carvings. My final cuts are done with a series of #2 and #3 gouges and a sharp detail knife. Leave the gouge marks so the finished project still looks like a carving after it's painted. Pay particular attention to the areas where two different colors will meet. Strive for crisp clean lines; fuzz causes problems when you try to get different colors of paint to meet along the borders. The small candy pieces in the backpack were carved separately and inserted after painting.

Painting and Finishing the Santa

I use undiluted acrylic paints to paint the Santa. Each color gets at least two coats; some colors may require three or more coats. I use flat shader brushes for everything except the tiny details. Keep painting until the colors are uniform. As a final touch-up, go back over the entire piece with a very small round detail brush and cover up any painting slips where two colors meet. Write the words on the sign with a fine-tip black permanent marker.

After the paint dries completely, antique and seal the piece. Dip the entire piece in dark walnut wood stain, then use an old towel to immediately wipe off as much stain as possible. Use some pressure and don't worry if a small amount of paint rubs off. The brisk rubbing helps develop a subdued shine. Let the piece dry thoroughly.

Mouth-watering details highlight this functional carving.

Candy Dish

Making the Candy Dish

Select your wood for the dish. The piece should be 2" thick. Use a band saw to shape the edges. I use a rotary power carver equipped with carbide burrs to remove most of the wood from inside the bowl and finish the inside with sandpaper. Start with 80-grit sandpaper and use progressively finer grits up to 400 grit. Remember to leave a small flat platform for Santa to stand on. If you plan to use the dish for unwrapped candies, use a finish that is compatible with food. I knew my dish would be used for wrapped candies so I use my favorite finish for hardwood: antique improver. Apply a heavy coat, allow it to soak in for five to ten minutes, then wipe away any excess. Apply a light coat the next day using the same procedure. Attach the Santa to the base with a wood screw.

Candy dish Santa patterns

Patterns are drawn to scale on a 1" grid. Enlarge or reduce to desired size.

(Sign reads: WILL CARVE FOR HERSHEY'S)

materials & tools

MATERIALS:
- 4" x 7" x 12" basswood (Santa)
- 1" x 3" x 3" basswood (Santa's backpack)
- 2" x 7" x 10" wood of choice (candy dish)
- Acrylic paints of choice (I use a variety of colors, but always use Napa red for Santa's coat)
- Dark walnut wood stain
- Antique improver
- Sandpaper, assorted grits up to 400 grit

TOOLS:
- Carving gouges of choice
- Detail knife
- Rotary power carver and large carbide bits
- Old towels
- Paintbrushes of choice
- Fine-tip black permanent marker

Secret Treasures Santa Claus

By Deborah Call

Santa climbing down the chimney with his bag full of presents makes a festive standalone carving. But this little Santa is more than a carving; he's hiding a secret! Santa's chimney doubles as a secret box. Simply hollow out the chimney to create a hidden box perfectly sized for holding small trinkets or a gift for that special someone.

Carving the Treasures Santa

Start by transferring the pattern to the wood. Cut straight across the top row of bricks with a band saw. Set the bottom half aside and cut one profile of the Santa top. Tape the cut-off pieces back onto the blank and cut the other profile. Then cut along the outline of the chimney-shaped box bottom.

Carve the Santa using your tools of choice. I've included a list of the tools I use. Continue re-drawing a centerline to keep things in perspective. I use a woodburner to add definition to Santa's beard. For the fur texture on Santa's hat and coat, I make small overlapping circles with a small round diamond bit in a rotary power carver.

Creating the Chimney Box

Measure and mark a 2¼" by 2¼" square centered on the top of the chimney blank. Determine the depth of the box. Leave enough wood so the bottom of the box is ½" thick. Mark the depth of the box cavity by wrapping tape around the largest drill bit you have. Drill a series of holes inside the square. Stop drilling when you reach the tape so you preserve the box bottom.

Use a ½" to ¾" #3 gouge to remove most of the waste wood inside the box. Use a ½"-wide single-bevel chisel to square up the corners and remove any rough edges. Shape the bottom of the box with a fine-grit cylinder-shaped carbide-point bit in a rotary power carver. Wrap a strip of fine-grit sandpaper around the sides and across the bottom of a small flat length of wood. Use the wood to provide the leverage needed to sand the sides, bottom, and corners of the box.

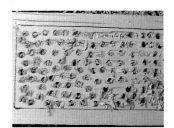 

Drill a series of holes to make it easy to hollow out the inside of the box.

Use a chisel or gouge to clear away the wood between the drilled holes.

Trace the brick pattern on the chimney and carve along the mortar lines with a 2mm U-gouge. Cut the lid insert to size. Use double-sided tape to secure the insert while you adjust the fit. When positioned properly, trace around the insert with a pencil. Glue the insert to the lid, wait a few minutes to let the wood glue begin to set, then clamp the insert to the lid using rubber bands.

Painting the Treasures Santa

Blend equal parts of Santa flesh and medium flesh with a small amount of matte varnish for Santa's face. Mix a very small amount of dusty mauve with the flesh color and varnish mixture. Use the dusty mauve mixture on Santa's cheeks, the tip of his nose, and just beneath the hat line. Paint the lips with dusty mauve.

Paint the beard with Quaker gray, then use a dry-brushing technique to highlight the beard and add depth. Paint the coat and hat with black cherry, the gloves with hunter green, and the bag with espresso. The holly leaves are hunter green with wedgwood green highlights.

Paint the mortar lines in the chimney Quaker gray. Then paint the bricks with barn red. For some of the bricks, add a little black or gray paint to change the color just a bit. Then dry brush a little Quaker gray over all of the bricks to age them a bit.

Finishing the Treasures Santa

Apply two coats of the matte varnish to prevent the piece from absorbing too much antiquing medium. Pick up a dab of blending gel along with a dab of antiquing medium on your paintbrush and coat one area at a time. The blending gel keeps the antiquing medium from drying too quickly. Wipe off the excess antiquing medium with a soft cloth. Use a clean dry paintbrush to remove the excess antiquing medium from hard-to-reach places. If Santa's beard looks too dark when the antiquing medium is dry, use a dry-brushing technique to lighten it up with white paint.

When the pieces are completely dry, apply a couple coats of matte varnish. Finish the inside of the box and the lid insert with tung oil varnish.

materials & tools

MATERIALS:
- 4" x 4" x 6" basswood
- ¼" x 2¼" x 2¼" basswood (lid insert)
- 500-grit sanding cloth

FINISHING MATERIALS:
- High-gloss tung oil finish
- Matte varnish
- Blending medium
- Brown antiquing medium

- Acrylic paints:
  Rich gold
  Silver
  Barn red
  Holly berry red
  Black cherry
  White
  Black
  Quaker gray
  Santa flesh
  Medium flesh
  Dusty mauve
  Light blue
  True blue

  Hunter green
  Wedgwood green
  Espresso

TOOLS:
- Carving knife
- Detail knife
- Drill and large drill bit
- Rotary power carver
- Fine-grit cylinder-shaped carbide-point bit
- #3 gouges: ⅛", ¼", ½", ¾"

- ½"-wide single-bevel chisel
- U-gouges: 1.5mm, 2mm
- Small round diamond bit
- Carving glove
- Thumb guard
- Band saw
- Woodburner
- Rubber bands

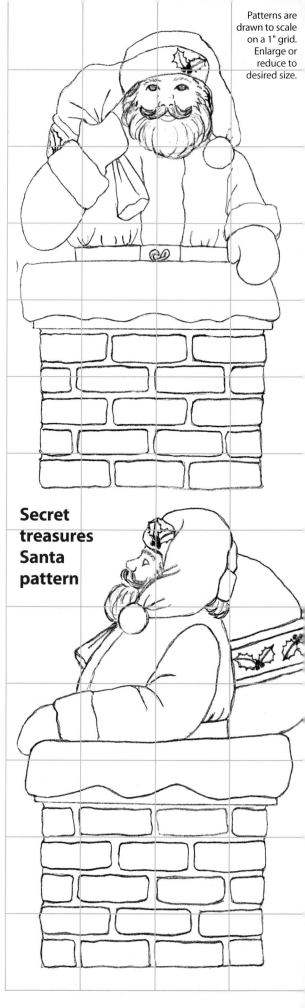

Patterns are drawn to scale on a 1" grid. Enlarge or reduce to desired size.

Secret treasures Santa pattern

Contributors

Robert Biermann
Robert, of Missouri, puts his decades of carving experience to use teaching.
twodulbug@sbcglobal.net
www.johnsworldofcarving.com

Vicki Bishop
Vicki, of Oklahoma, has been carving since 1999 . She and her husband, Phil, have taught seminars all over the country.
bishop7333@sbcglobal.net
www.bishopwoodcarving.com

Steve Brown
Steve, of Kentucky, enjoys carving caricature and realistic figures. He wrote two carving books and conducts several seminars a year.
sbrownwoodcarvin@bellsouth.net
www.sbrownwoodcarving.com

Deborah Call
Deborah, of Pennsylvania, is a self-taught woodcarver inspired by everyday life. She carves more Santas than anything else.
www.deborahcall.com

Shawn Cipa
Shawn, of Pennsylvania, is a professional carver who has written five carving books for Fox Chapel.
www.shawnscarvings.com

Don Dearolf
Don, of Pennsylvania, painted for several years before taking up carving in 1994 after attending a local carving show.

Jim Feather
Jim, of Pennsylvania, has been carving for more than three decades and enjoys caricature and teaching carving.

Mark Gargac
Mark, of Colorado, is an HVAC contractor and semi-professional woodcarver and instructor.
www.gargacsoriginals.com

Dan Haack
Dan, of Wisconsin, took up woodcarving after becoming disabled in 2000. He teaches woodcarving to Boy Scouts and students at U.W. Wisconsin School of the Arts.
danwoodcarver@gmail.com

Desiree Hajny
Desiree, of Nebraska, has written a number of books on carving for Fox Chapel and has taught across North America.
hajny@gtmc.net

Forrest Holder
Forrest, of Tennessee, has been carving since 2006. He is a self-taught carver.
www.tnartist05.blogspot.com

Rick Jensen
Rick, of Minnesota, is an internationally-known carver, author, and instructor. He co-authored *The Illustrated Guide to Carving Tree Bark* for Fox Chapel.
jrjensen@gvtel.com

Ron Johnson
Ron, of Alabama, began carving and joined the National Woodcarving Association in 1972. He enjoys exchanging Santa pencils.
robojo222@yahoo.com

Cyndi Joslyn
Cyndi, of Indiana, is a Santa collector and carver. She teaches carving and has written several carving books for Fox Chapel.
cyndijoslyn@gmail.com

Bob Mason
Bob, of Missouri, has been carving for more than three decades. He enjoys displaying and selling his art.

Jim McGuire
Jim, of North Carolina, retired from the pharmaceutical manufacturing industry in 2005 and became a full-time woodcarver and sculptor.
www.wilsonwoodcarvers.com

Paul McLeod
Paul, of Arkansas, retired from the faculty of The University of Arkansas at Little Rock in 1998. He enjoys teaching and attending carving classes.
www.whiterivercrafts.com

Hugh Parks
Hugh, of Canada, started carving duck decoys in 1987 and started carving professionally in 1998.
www.feathersinwood.com

Floyd Rhadigan
Floyd, of Michigan, is president of the Caricature Carvers of America. He enjoys teaching seminars.
www.fantasycarving.com

Kathleen Schuck
Kathleen, of Idaho, began carving in 1950 and owned and operated a carving store for eighteen years. She retired in 2004, but has continued to teach carving.

Jim Sebring
Jim, of Pennsylvania, has been carving in the tramp-art style since 1995. His work has been on display in many historic venues.

Wayne Shinlever
Wayne, of Tennessee, is a retired police officer who now carves and teaches carving full-time.
www.carvingsbywayne.com

Arnold Smith
Arnold, of Georgia, is retired from Warner Robins Air Force Base. He worked with the Museum of Aviation and won many awards for his work as a display specialist.

Sandy Smith
Sandy, of Arkansas, is active in the North Arkansas Woodcarvers Club.
www.northarkansaswoodcarvers.org

Doug Stewart
Doug, of Kansas, started carving at age ten. A high school teacher, he also coaches football and girls' basketball.
dstewart@usd244ks.org

Don Swartz
Don, of Pennsylvania, owns a carving supply store and teaches carving.
carvingtherapy@gmail.com

John Zanzalari
John, of New Jersey, taught himself to carve in 1987 and hasn't stopped since. His carvings are in private collections across the United States and England. He retired from the Chubb Corporation.

Index

More Great Project Books from Fox Chapel Publishing

The Best of WOODCARVING ILLUSTRATED

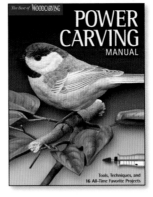

Power Carving Manual
Tools, Tecnhniques, and 16 All-Time Favorite Projects
By Editors of *Woodcarving Illustrated*

Everything you need to know about power carving! From the pages of *Woodcarving Illustrated* come projects for a folk art Santa, an engraved gunstock, and more.

ISBN: 978-1-56523-450-5
$19.95 • 144 Pages

Woodcarver's Guide to Sharpening, Tools and Setting Up Shop
Expert Tips and Techniques
By Editors of *Woodcarving Illustrated*

The best tips and tricks from the pages of *Woodcarving Illustrated*, this guidebook provides you with all you need to know to create a safe and organized workshop and employ various tools.

ISBN: 978-1-56523-475-8
$19.95 • 144 Pages

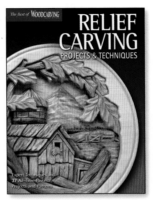

Relief Carving Projects & Techniques
Expert Advice and 37 All-Time Favorite Projects and Patterns
By Editors of *Woodcarving Illustrated*

Tried and true relief woodcarving projects and patterns to create an assortment of compelling carvings for the home and beyond.

ISBN: 978-1-56523-558-8
$19.95 • 144 Pages

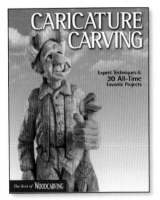

Caricature Carving
Expert Techniques & 30 All-Time Favorite Projects
By Editors of *Woodcarving Illustrated*

Have fun creating amusing figures with ideas, expert techniques and tips collected in this great reference book of projects from the editors of *Woodcarving Illustrated*.

ISBN: 978-1-56523-474-1
$19.95 • 144 Pages

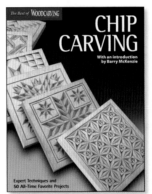

Chip Carving
Expert Techniques and 50 All-Time Favorite Projects
By Editors of *Woodcarving Illustrated*

Take a journey into this old-world art form. Discover patterns, tips, and techniques, as well as a beautiful gallery of work to spur the imagination for unique creations.

ISBN: 978-1-56523-449-9
$19.95 • 128 Pages

WOODCARVING
ILLUSTRATED MAGAZINE

In addition to being a leading source of woodworking books and DVDs, Fox Chapel also publishes *Woodcarving Illustrated*. Released quarterly, it delivers premium projects, expert tips and techniques from today's finest carvers, and in-depth information about the latest tools, equipment, and materials.

Subscribe Today!
Woodcarving Illustrated: **888-506-6630**
www.woodcarvingillustrated.com

Look For These Books at Your Local Bookstore or Woodworking Retailer
To order direct, call **800-457-9112** or visit *www.FoxChapelPublishing.com*

By mail, please send check or money order to:

# Item	Shipping Rate	
1 Item	$3.99 US	$8.98 CAN
Each Additional	.99 US	$3.99 CAN

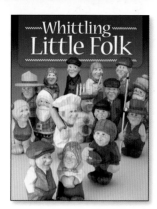

Whittling Little Folk

*20 Delightful Characters
to Carve and Paint*

By Harley Refsal

A single carving knife and an afternoon is all that is needed to create one of the charming little characters in this book.

ISBN: 978-1-56523-518-2
$16.95 • 128 Pages

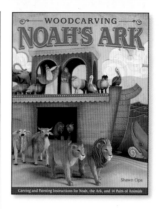

Woodcarving Noah's Ark

*Carving and Painting Instructions
for the Noah, the Ark, and 14 Pairs
of Animals*

By Shawn Cipa

Recreate the amazing adventure of Noah's Ark with a hand-carved wooden set that will be cherished for generations.

ISBN: 978-1-56523-477-2
$22.95 • 160 Pages

Lettering & Sign Carving Workbook

*10 Skill-Building Projects for Carving
and Painting Custom Signs*

By Betty Padden

A contemporary look at a nostalgic craft with updated techniques and a fresh variety of styles for carving and painting signs for the home, summer cottage or basement bar.

ISBN: 978-1-56523-452-9
$19.95 • 160 Pages

Woodcarving the Nativity in Folk Art Style

*Step-by-Step Instructions
and Patterns for a 15-Piece
Manger Scene*

By Shawn Cipa

ISBN: 978-1-56523-202-0
$14.95 • 88 Pages

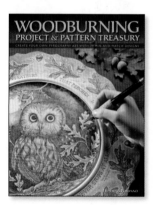

Woodburning Project & Pattern Treasury

*70 Mix and Match Designs to Create
Your Own Pyrography Art*

By Deborah Pompano

A fresh take on the craft of woodburning focusing on the drawing, lettering, and design elements that when learned will add dimension and composition to any pyrography project.

ISBN: 978-1-56523-482-6
$24.95 • 176 Pages

Carving Santas from Around the World

*15 Quick and Easy Projects
to Make and Give*

By Cyndi Joslyn

Find 15 ready-to-carve Santas from around the world with 2 step-by-step projects featuring a Traditional Santa and England's Father Christmas.

ISBN: 978-1-56523-187-0
$14.95 • 96 Pages

Illustrated Guide to Carving Tree Bark

*Releasing Whimsical Houses &
Woodspirits from Found Wood*

By Rick Jensen and Jack A. Williams

Carving found wood has never been easier with step-by-step instructions for releasing whimsical bark animals, wood spirits, Santas, and more.

ISBN: 978-1-56523-218-1
$14.95 • 80 Pages

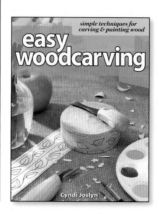

Easy Woodcarving

*Simple Techniques for
Carving & Painting Wood*

By Cyndi Joslyn

ISBN: 978-1-56523-288-4
$14.95 • 152 Pages

Look For These Books at Your Local Bookstore or Woodworking Retailer

To order direct, call **800-457-9112** or visit *www.FoxChapelPublishing.com*

By mail, please please send check or money order to:

# Item	Shipping Rate	
1 Item	$3.99 US	$8.98 CAN
Each Additional	.99 US	$3.99 CAN